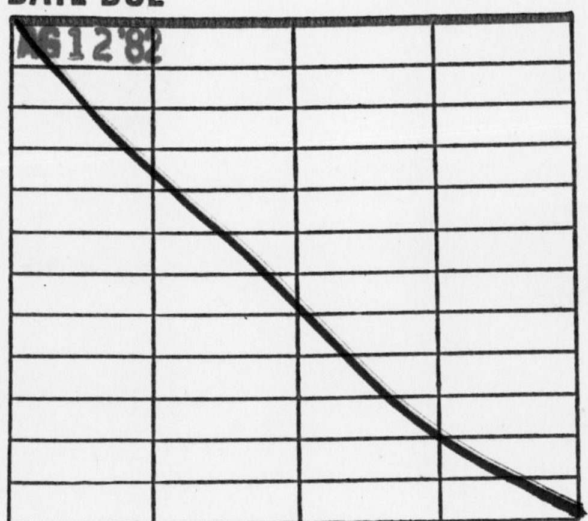
DATE DUE
AG 12 '82

# SOVIET FOREIGN POLICY
# 1917–1941

GEORGE F. KENNAN

*Institute for Advanced Study*
*Princeton, New Jersey*

AN ANVIL ORIGINAL

*under the general editorship of*

LOUIS L. SNYDER

D. VAN NOSTRAND COMPANY

New York Cincinnati Toronto London Melbourne

This book is dedicated to Mr. Louis Fischer
in recognition of his unique contribution
to the history of Soviet foreign policy

---

D. Van Nostrand Company Regional Offices:
*New York Cincinnati Milbrae*

D. Van Nostrand Company International Offices:
*London Toronto Melbourne*



ISBN: 0-442-00047-2



Published by D. Van Nostrand Company
450 West 33rd Street, New York, N. Y. 10001

Published simultaneously in Canada by
Van Nostrand Reinhold Ltd.

15 14 13 12 11 10 9 8

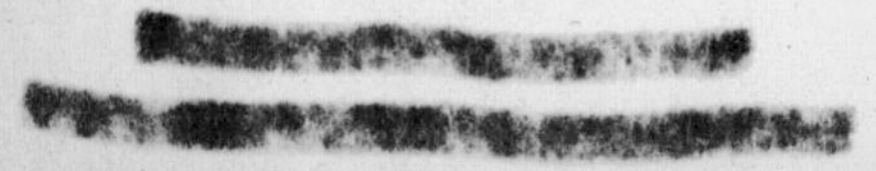

# PREFACE

The purpose of this treatise is to give a brief account of Soviet foreign policy from the moment of the Bolshevik seizure of power in 1917 to the involvement of the Soviet Union in the Second World War, in June 1941.

The history of Soviet foreign *policy* should not be confused with a history of Soviet foreign *relations*. It is not the purpose here to illuminate, any further than is necessary to an understanding of Soviet behavior, the motives and actions of other governments in their relations with the Soviet Union. The purpose is rather to explore the motives and calculations from which the Soviet leaders acted, the nature of the policies they pursued, and the significance of the major actions they performed pursuant to these policies. For this reason the accompanying documentation is restricted in the main to items illustrating the Soviet view.

It would be impossible to list all of those friends and colleagues, both in the academic profession and in government, to whom I am indebted for stimulus and insights of one sort or another which have helped me in this study. A special debt of gratitude must be recorded at once to Mr. Louis Fischer. His views on these matters need no reflection in anyone else's work and find none in this. But I have drawn copiously on the unique resources of his *The Soviets in World Affairs, 1917-1929,* and he has stood at my side during the writing and has given generously of his deep knowledge of this subject. Of the other secondary works which I have exploited without compunction in putting together this account, I must mention particularly the excellent study of Soviet foreign policy in the 1930's by Professor Max Beloff, the many works of Professor E. H. Carr, whose outstanding contribution to the history of the Soviet Union has left every student of Soviet affairs in his debt, and the great labor of William Langer and S. Everett Gleason in straightening out the tangled tale of world affairs in the period 1939 to 1941. A debt must also be acknowledged to my friend

Gustav Hilger and his collaborator, Alfred G. Meyer, for their balanced and useful account of German-Soviet relations of the years to which this study is addressed.

As for the documentary section, I must at once pass on a considerable share of the credit for the unearthing and translation of this set of documents to Mrs. Jane Degras and her associates at the Royal Institute of International Affairs. Being unable to improve on the well-selected and well-prepared translations of her three volumes of documents on Soviet foreign policy and the companion volumes of documents on the Communist International, I have drawn on them for eight of the items included in this collection. A similar special indebtedness must be acknowledged to Madame Xenia Youkoff Eudin and Professor Harold H. Fisher, of the Hoover Library at Stanford, California, whose services generally to the study of recent Russian history no scholar can mention without a sense of warmest appreciation. Four of the documents in this volume are taken from the excellent and highly useful documentary survey, *Soviet Russia and the West, 1920-1927*.

Grateful acknowledgment is also made for the use of four excerpts reprinted from *Soviet Russia and the West, 1920-1927,* by Xenia Joukoff Eudin and Harold H. Fisher with the permission of the publishers, Stanford University Press, Copyright 1957 by the Board of Trustees of Leland Stanford Junior University; for the use of three excerpts reprinted from *The Communist International, 1919-1943, Documents,* Vol. I, edited by Jane Degras and published by the Oxford University Press in 1956 on behalf of the Royal Institute of International Affairs; for the use of five excerpts reprinted from the three volumes of *Soviet Documents on Foreign Policy,* edited by Jane Degras and published in 1951, 1952, and 1953 by the Oxford University Press on behalf of the Royal Institute of International Affairs; and for the use of the text of the Rapallo Treaty reprinted from *Soviet Treaty Series,* Vol. I, edited by Leonard Shapiro and published in 1950 by the Georgetown University Press, Washington, D.C.

*Princeton, New Jersey* G.F.K.
*May 1960*

# TABLE OF CONTENTS

# Part I

# SOVIET FOREIGN POLICY, 1917-1941

## — 1 —

# INTRODUCTION

No one familiar with the history of Soviet foreign policy would fail to feel a sense of trepidation in undertaking to give in the space of 115 pages a chronological account of what transpired in this vast field of activity over the 24 eventful years from 1917 to 1941. I have had occasion to record, in the preface to another historical work, the belief that the history of diplomacy is of such complexity that it often becomes fully intelligible only when examined in minute detail. What is attempted in this present volume is unavoidably in conflict with this principle. Every paragraph is, of necessity, an exercise in the simplification of the complicated. The omissions are necessarily many; and not all scholars will agree with the decisions they reflect as to what to include and what to omit.

Yet the fact that the effort has been undertaken at all reflects the author's belief that a summary of this nature has its place in the historical literature about Soviet foreign policy. The original documentation on this subject, though far from complete, is already enormous; and not all of it is available in English. Few nonspecialists will have the leisure, the competence, and the interest to undertake an independent study of it, or even to go through the major secondary works in which various segments of this history are treated. For those who cannot perform this labor but would nevertheless like to have some idea of how the conduct of Soviet foreign policy proceeded in the years before Russia became a focal point of western attention, this brief summary may have its uses. And the accompanying documents, replete as they are with references and implications which no commentary of this length could fully clarify, may serve at least to give the reader a sense of that curious intellectual and semantic atmosphere in which the formulation of Soviet foreign policy has at all times proceeded, and in the light of which, alone, it becomes—in most instances, if not all—intelligible.

— 2 —

# THE WORLD WAR AND THE BEGINNINGS OF THE INTERVENTION

To understand the principal motives by which the leaders of the Russian Communist (Bolshevik) Party were guided as they took up the reins of government in the Russian capital of Petrograd in November 1917, it is necessary to take account of two outstanding features of their political position, as of that moment.

**The Relationship of the Russian Revolution to World Revolution.** It will be recalled that Lenin and his associates were the beneficiaries of a series of dramatic and wholly unexpected events which had carried them, in the space of a few short months of 1917, from the status of obscure political exiles to that of the dictatorial rulers of most of Russia. Pleased and surprised as they were by this extraordinary turn of fortune, they did not consider that by seizing power in Russia they had in any sense achieved their goal, even to the extent of producing there the socialist revolution to which they aspired. They did not believe, in fact, that this revolution *could* be carried to completion in Russia alone. They viewed, as essential to the achievement even of their program in Russia, the prior accomplishment of a real socialist revolution in at least one of the great industrial countries of western Europe; and it was particularly to Germany that their eyes turned in this connection.

But it was not just *for the sake of* revolution in Russia that the Russian communists yearned for revolution in

Germany and elsewhere in the West. They were internationalists—the disciples of a German theorist, Karl Marx, whose views had not even been primarily relevant to Russia. It was precisely *revolution in the leading industrial countries of Europe* that constituted the main target of Bolshevik hopes and strivings in 1917—and this not for the sake of Russia but for its own sake. Western Europe, in their view, was more important than Russia. The principal significance of the revolution that had just taken place in Russia was seen by its authors to lie in its quality as a prelude to that collapse of all European imperialism in which they were primarily interested.

Thus, great as was their satisfaction over what had occurred in Russia, and determined as they were to cling to and strengthen the important position of power they had now gained there, the final prospering of their purposes depended, as they saw it, on the early spread of the revolution to other countries of Europe. It was to this that their principal hopes and efforts were directed as they turned to the exercise of their new responsibilities as Russia's rulers.

**The Bolsheviki and the World War.** Throughout the earlier years of the World War then in progress, Lenin had been, among the European socialists, the outstanding advocate of an international socialist position which repudiated the war as a whole. The Leninist position was based on a view of the war aims of both contending coalitions as being equally unworthy, hypocritical, and rapacious. It required all good socialists to adopt a position of defeatism and to oppose the war efforts of their own countries. It called, in fact, for revolutionary action by the proletariat in all the warring countries, designed to turn the existing "imperialist" war into a series of civil wars.

It is important to recognize that Lenin, while calling for an end to the European war, did not want peace for abstract or humanitarian reasons. He did not particularly want peace at all unless it should be accompanied by socialist revolutions.

Now, in his new position as head of the Russian state, Lenin could not possibly take responsibility for continuing Russia's participation in a war he had always opposed and had urged others to oppose. He was deeply committed, by his past record and political position, to take Russia out of the war. But here he found himself in difficulty. It was clear that it would be dangerous and difficult for Russia to leave the war alone. Russia was now militarily helpless. The communists had deliberately promoted the disintegration of the old Russian army as a means of facilitating their own seizure of power. It was already impossible to reconstitute Russia's fighting capacity, even had one wished to do so. Unless the peace should be a general one, embracing all the warring parties, or unless a revolution should take place in Germany which would alter the entire foreign and military policy of that country, the Germans could be expected to take advantage of this momentary weakness of Russia in order to impose an onerous settlement, which might well crush the Soviet government.

Everything thus depended, from Lenin's standpoint, on immediate action to cause a general cessation of hostilities rather than a separate one between Germany and Russia, and to see that it was accompanied, if not preceded, by decisive revolutionary action on the part of the workers of the western countries. These two things—peace and revolution—were intimately linked in Lenin's mind. A peace without revolution could be expected to lead merely to a reconciliation among the various member-states of the western capitalist world, and to the formation of a common front against the Russian revolution. This would be worse than no peace at all. World revolution, on the other hand, as Lenin conceived it and hoped for it, would necessarily mean peace; for it would bring to power people who, like himself, had only contempt for the issues over which the war was ostensibly being waged, and who would at once agree to a general cessation of hostilities.

**The Bolshevik Peace Move.** In these circumstances, it was no more than natural—indeed, it was an urgent necessity—for the Bolshevik leaders to begin their conduct of Russia's foreign relations by issuing to the peoples of the world an appeal calling for an immediate cessation of hostilities. Such an appeal was indeed put forward, in the form of the celebrated Decree on Peace (*see Document No. 1*), approved on the very day of the revolution by the Second All-Russian Congress of Soviets of Workers', Soldiers', and Peasants' Deputies. It was reaffirmed in several later pronouncements and communications of the Soviet government.

While this peace appeal unquestionably increased restlessness and yearning for peace in some circles of the western labor movement, it failed of its central purpose. It produced, immediately, neither revolution nor peace. The authority of the other warring governments remained unshaken. Not one of them showed itself prepared to join in the move for a general cessation of hostilities. The Bolsheviki had no choice, therefore, but to enter into independent negotiations with the Germans, first for an armistice and then, reluctantly, in the last days of December 1917, for a separate peace.

**The Brest-Litovsk Negotiations.** The German-Russian negotiations took place at the German military headquarters at Brest-Litovsk. The talks proceeded, with interruptions, from December 20, 1917, to February 10, 1918. On the side of the Central Powers there were represented, in addition to Germany, Austria-Hungary, Bulgaria, and Turkey. It soon became evident that the German High Command was determined that Russian Poland as well as the Baltic provinces of Kurland and Lithuania should be separated from Russia and their fate reserved for settlement by the German government. In addition to this, the Germans were unwilling to recognize the authority of the Soviet government as extending to the Ukraine; and they insisted on entering into separate peace negotiations with the representatives of a Ukrainian separatist regime, the so-called Rada, which, with its seat at Kiev, was still defying Soviet authority by force of arms on a portion of Ukrainian territory. It was evident, in view of the military helplessness of the Rada and the importance to the German-Austrian war effort of the food supplies and other resources of the Ukraine, that the conclusion of such a treaty between the Germans and the Rada would not only prejudice the chances of the Bolsheviki for establishing their power in that area but would be rapidly followed by the effective German occupation of the Ukraine.

These German demands thus constituted a serious blow to Soviet hopes and prospects in the Russian domestic-political field, and posed a bitter problem for the Soviet leadership. Sharp dissension at once arose in the higher ranks of the Party. Lenin favored acceptance of the German demands. (*See Document No. 2.*) Some members of his entourage favored their defiant rejection, followed by an attempt to conduct a "revolutionary" war against the German government. Others, among them Trotsky, favored an intermediate position by which the Soviet government, while declining to continue hostilities, also disdained to sign the imposed peace. It was in pursuance of this latter concept that Trotsky, as head of the Soviet delegation, broke off the talks on February 10, refusing to accept the German terms. The German reaction was to resume hostilities and to begin a further military advance onto Russian territory. Even the hotheads and romanticists in the Party were now obliged to recognize the logic of Lenin's position. In great agony of spirit, the decision was taken to capitulate. On March 3, Soviet negotiators put their signature to a new set of German terms, even more drastic than those they had declined to sign before the renewed German offensive.[1] This document, known as the Treaty of Brest-Litovsk, was ratified on March 15 by a special (fourth) session of the highest body of the Soviet government, the Congress of Soviets.

Although the Ukrainian Rada had been driven out of Kiev, and its authority crushed, by Soviet forces in early February, just at the time of the signature of the separate German-Ukrainian treaty, the Germans continued to regard this treaty as being in effect. Basing themselves on its terms, they immediately proceeded to a military occupation of the entire Ukraine, forcing the Soviet units to withdraw and reinstating the Rada, initially, as a puppet regime. (Later, when the Rada had proved too incompetent administratively to serve as a useful agency for the German procurement of food and raw materials in the Ukraine, the Germans replaced it with a more subservient and conservative puppet government under the Hetman Skoropadsky.)

In signing and ratifying the peace of Brest-Litovsk, the

[1] Turkey, in particular, as an ally of Germany in the war, exploited the helplessness of the Russians at that moment by demanding, and obtaining, in the final Brest-Litovsk settlement, the cession of the city of Batum as well as of two districts, Kars and Ardagan, along the Russo-Turkish border.

Soviet government had at first very little confidence that the Germans would respect the treaty. They themselves intended to respect it only so far as circumstances necessitated. In the weeks that followed ratification of the treaty, up to the arrival of the first German Ambassador, Count Mirbach, on April 23, the Soviet leaders lived in constant fear of another renewal of military operations by the Germans. One result of this anxiety was the removal of the seat of government from Petrograd, which was particularly vulnerable to seizure by the Germans, to the ancient and historical capital of Moscow, which lay farther in the interior and was in less immediate danger. The Germans, for their part, generally respected the specific territorial provisions of the treaty, which related only to the western boundary of Russia north of the Ukraine. But they continued to refuse to recognize the right of the Soviet government to have any voice in the affairs of the Ukraine. The authority of the Soviet government was thus effectively confined, in this initial period, to northern European Russia and Siberia.

**The Effect of Brest-Litovsk on the Allies.** This series of events in the relationship of Russia to the war and to the Germans naturally caused greatest consternation and anxiety to the western Allies, particularly the French and British, who at that time still bore almost exclusive responsibility for the conduct of the war in the West. The collapse of the Russian army and Russia's formal withdrawal from the war meant that the Germans would be able to move to the western front, in time for the offensive they were plainly preparing to launch there in the spring of 1918, the bulk of the German forces which had theretofore been engaged in the East. Obviously, this would mean a major and, for the Allies, extremely dangerous alteration in the balance of forces on the western front.

The Soviet leaders had no particular desire to see this displacement of German forces occur. To be sure, their own military helplessness was so great that it made little difference to them in the military sense whether the Germans had 2,500,000 or 250,000 men in the East. But they did not want to incur in the eyes of the workers of the Allied countries the onus of having, if only inadvertently, greatly improved the position of the Germans in the war. They therefore made an effort, in the initial armistice negotiations, to get the Germans to agree to a clause barring the transfer of troops from one front to another. But there was no real possibility of dissuading the Germans to desist from a move of such overwhelming importance to their own war effort. The best the Russians could achieve was the inclusion in the armistice agreement of an ambiguous and meaningless clause, under the cover of which the Germans proceeded, in the course of the autumn and winter of 1917-1918, to move some forty divisions, comprising a total of approximately 2,000,000 men, from the eastern to the western front.

Responsible leaders in the Allied camp, both military and civil, at once cast around for means by which to combat this trend of events. The minds of some turned to the possibility of Allied military intervention in Russia, designed to restore resistance to Germany in the East either by direct military action or by supporting the re-establishment in Russia of a government loyal to the Allied war effort. Others favored a policy of supporting, and collaborating with, the Soviet regime, with a view to stiffening its position vis-à-vis the Germans and enabling it to offer such resistance to German pressures as would force the Germans to maintain substantial forces in Russia and the Ukraine. One faction, in other words, wanted to restore resistance to Germany in the East by working *against* the Soviet government (for this is what was implied by any military intervention without Soviet consent); the other faction wanted to restore it by working *with* the Soviet government. Still others, notably Woodrow Wilson, hoped that the formulation and announcement by the Allied governments of a more liberal and inspiring concept of war aims would serve to rally Russia once more, whether under Soviet or some other leadership, to the Allied cause. Wilson's famous "Fourteen Points" speech, of January 8, 1918, was an attempt to realize this hope.

**The Possibility of Allied Military Aid to the Soviet Government.** The idea of getting Russia to oppose Germany by giving direct military aid to the Soviet government was most prominently and vigorously represented by certain of the unofficial, or semi-official, Allied representatives in Russia.[2] During, and immediately after, the crisis in the Brest-Litovsk talks, these men were encouraged, particularly by Trotsky (Commissar for Foreign Affairs up to about the time of the decision to sign the Brest-Litovsk Treaty, and thereafter Commissar for War), to hope that if the Allies would only restrain the Japanese from intervening in Siberia and would promise military aid, the Soviet government would defy the Germans and would endeavor, with Allied assistance, to mount some sort of resistance to German encroachments. (*See Document No. 3.*) Naturally, the unofficial Allied agents were excited over this possibility and did their best to get their governments to pursue it.

Trotsky's reasons for encouraging such hopes lay in the highly confused conditions of the moment. Lenin and the majority of his associates in the Central Committee were prepared in principle to accept Allied aid only in the event that the Germans refused to accept the Soviet capitulation or, having accepted it, failed to respect the treaty and accordingly continued the military advance into Russia with a view to crushing the Soviet regime. It was these possible contingencies (neither of which ever actually materialized) and only these, that Lenin had in mind when he declared himself, when pressed by his colleagues, as in favor of "accepting arms and potatoes from the bandits of Anglo-French imperialism." Besides, the Soviet leaders acutely feared that the Japanese would take advantage of this, their own moment of maximum weakness and difficulty, in order to intervene in Siberia; and they hoped that by dangling before the western Allied governments the possibility of renewed resistance to Germany, they could cause the latter to put a restraining hand on the Japanese.

Actually, these hopes for Allied military aid to the Soviet government were short-lived. The failure of the Germans to renew the offensive removed whatever reality such calculations might have had in Soviet policy; and the

[2] These were, particularly, Mr. Bruce Lockhart, official British agent in Russia; Mr. Raymond Robins, head of the American Red Cross Commission in Russia; and M. Jacques Sadoul, a member of the French Military Mission there.

idea never did commend itself to the higher Allied military authorities in Paris and London, whose approval would have been requisite to its realization. After the opening of the great German offensive on the western front, on March 21, 1918, the desperation of the French and British military planners at the Supreme War Council in Versailles was such that they were disinclined to reckon with the uncertainties of possible Soviet "consent," and favored any kind of military intervention in Russia that could conceivably be arranged, and as soon as possible. Once the new German diplomatic mission had arrived in Moscow in late April, French and British policy swung rapidly and decisively in the direction of a unilateral Allied intervention, regardless of the Soviet attitude.

**The Beginnings of Allied Intervention.** There were, at that time, only two places where the Allies could intervene in Russia. One was through the ports of the Russian North, Murmansk and Archangel; the other, through Vladivostok. The French and British had almost no troops to spare for an action at either point. The whole project depended on the United States and the Japanese being willing to put up the bulk of the forces. The higher officials of the United States government were at all times skeptical of the possible value of such undertakings, and were initially most reluctant to give them their collaboration or encouragement. They were particularly reluctant to encourage any unilateral Japanese intervention in Siberia, and were therefore disinclined to support any such undertaking economically and financially. The Japanese, for their part, hesitated to involve themselves in any major action in Siberia unless they had assurance both of American economic and financial support, on the one hand, and of full freedom, on the other, to act alone and in pursuit of their own national interests as they saw them. Obviously, these various positions conflicted; and for this reason the project of intervention on a major scale hung fire through the first six months of 1918.

During this period, however, minor actions occurred which greatly inflamed Soviet suspicions. On April 5, the Japanese, pleading the necessity of protecting their citizens, and acting without prior consultation with Washington, landed a small force of marines in Vladivostok.

The British at once followed suit. The Soviet government of course protested violently. (*See Document No. 4.*) At Murmansk, furthermore, where the local soviet was particularly friendly to the Allies and where matters were complicated by the civil war in adjacent Finland (in relation to which the Allies and the Soviet authorities had certain common interests), an intimate collaboration grew up between the local soviet and the Allied naval forces stationed in the port. British marines were landed there as early as March, by agreement with the Murmansk Soviet, to help preserve order in the community.

The Soviet leaders in Moscow at first observed without strong protest the growth of this collaboration between the Allies and the local Soviet authorities in Murmansk, because they were not yet certain that they might not at some point require Allied aid against the Germans. But as the spring of 1918 wore on, as the prospects for another German attack diminished, and as the influence of the Allies at Murmansk began to rival their own, the suspicion and resentment of the Soviet leaders in Moscow increased. Relations between Moscow and the Murmansk Soviet finally deteriorated, at the end of June, to the point of a complete political break. This left Murmansk in effect under Allied occupation, and in a virtual state of war with the central Soviet authorities.

At about this time, President Wilson was finally persuaded by the Allies (largely through the direct intervention of the Allied commander on the western front, Marshal Ferdinand Foch) to contribute American forces for a mixed Allied expedition to North Russia, under British command. Without awaiting the arrival of the Americans, a British and French advance party moved, on August 2, to seize Archangel, the largest port in the Russian North and still in Soviet hands. With the help of anticommunist agents ashore, the port was easily seized, the Soviet garrison expelled, and a defensive perimeter established about a hundred miles in radius around the city. In September, the expedition was reinforced by the arrival of the three American battalions.

The British hope was that this action would make possible the recruitment of an anti-Bolshevik armed force in the Archangel area, which could form the nucleus of a new noncommunist political movement, loyal to the

Allies. So great was the optimism of the British in this respect that the entire operation was put in hand with a force numbering only a few thousand men, wholly inadequate for the occupation of any extensive area of Russian territory.

As for Siberia, the situation there was changed in the late spring of 1918 by the uprising against Soviet authority of several tens of thousands of Czech troops[3] who were in transit through Siberia in the direction of Vladivostok, hoping to sail from there for the western front. The rebelling Czechs were at once joined by anticommunist Russian factions. This event led to the collapse of Soviet power and the temporary triumph of various "White" (anti-Soviet) factions, throughout most of Siberia. It also gave great encouragement to those elements in the western countries who favored intervention.

Woodrow Wilson, who understood poorly the complexities of the Siberian situation but had a sentimental sympathy for the Czechoslovak independence movement, was now finally moved to propose a joint American-Japanese action, the purpose of which he naïvely conceived as assistance to the Czechs. The Japanese accepted the proposal in principle, but did so of course for purposes of their own which had nothing to do with the rescue of the Czechs. The result was the despatch to Siberia, in August and September 1918, of about ten thousand American troops and several tens of thousands of Japanese. Between them, the Japanese and the Americans took control of most of the Trans-Siberian Railway east of Lake Baikal. The Japanese also took advantage of this development to establish themselves firmly in northern Manchuria.

**The Soviet Reaction to the Initial Acts of Intervention.** The Soviet government was of course tremendously exercised over these events of the summer and autumn of 1918, particularly because they were coincidental with a series of efforts made by the opponents of Soviet power to unseat or assassinate the Soviet leaders. They suspected

[3] This Czech force, often known as the "Czech Corps" or the "Czechoslovak Legion," was composed partly of Austro-Hungarian war prisoners of Czech nationality who had gone over to the Allied cause, and partly of young men from the Czech colonies in Russia.

with some justification (though they exaggerated its intensity and efficiency) collusion between the French and British and the internal enemies of Bolshevism. Their bitterness over this factor was extreme and lasting. On the other hand, they were both pleased and puzzled to learn of the absurd inadequacy of the force that had been sent to North Russia. They proceeded at once to institute vigorous military opposition both to the Czechs and the noncommunist Russian forces in Siberia and to the Allied forces at Murmansk and at Archangel. These events marked the real beginning of the Russian civil war.

The Allied forces had scarcely arrived in Siberia and North Russia when the World War ended (November 11). The German collapse occasioned the withdrawal both of the German diplomatic mission in Russia and of the German occupying forces in the Ukraine. It put an end, of course, to the whole complex of problems which had arisen for Soviet diplomacy by virtue of the fact that the war was in progress. But it left the Allies with forces, newly arrived, on Russian soil, for whose presence there the rationale of opposition to the Germans had now ceased to have any validity. Only now, for the first time, could the question of Soviet relations with the major western powers be faced by both sides without the confusing factor that had been present, during the first year of Soviet power, in the form of the world war still in progress in the West.

— 3 —

# INTERVENTION AND CIVIL WAR

**Implications of the End of the World War.** The events of early November 1918—notably the termination of hostilities in the World War and the revolution by which this event was accompanied in Germany—had several connotations of highest importance to the Soviet leaders.

First of all, military collapse in Germany relieved them of the German occupation of the Ukraine and of the greatest military threat which had theretofore confronted them.

Secondly, the revolution in Germany, marked as it was by the mutiny at Kiel and the fall of the monarchy, appeared to their somewhat egocentric vision as the obvious counterpart of Russia's "February" revolution, and set up in their minds the most eager hopes that it would soon be followed by a German "October." [1]

Thirdly, the end of hostilities in the West, removing as it did the main ostensible reason for the Allied intervention in Russia, permitted the hope that the Allies might now be moved to withdraw their troops from Russia. In the civil war within Russia, things were by this time progressing relatively favorably, from the communist standpoint. Trotsky, as Commissar for War, was having conspicuous success in whipping into shape a new Soviet armed force, adequate at least for the limited and relatively primitive demands of this internal conflict. The domestic opponents of Bolshevism had now been revealed as hopelessly disunited. That element among these opponents (the monarchists and ex-officers) which had a near monopoly of the military and administrative skills was fatally lacking in popular support. The rival element —the moderate socialists (Mensheviki and the moderate and Right-Wing Social-Revolutionaries)—had wide support among the peasantry but lacked experience in administrative and military leadership. These two factions were divided from each other by suspicions and resentments no smaller than those which divided both of them from the Bolsheviki. Their inability to work together hampered most fatefully their capacity to resist the communists. By November 1918 it was already evident that without extensive foreign military support, the White (anti-Bolshevik) cause would fail and the Bolsheviki

[1] The reference here is of course to the two Russian revolutions of 1917: the moderate-liberal one, usually referred to in Russian usage as the "February Revolution," and the Bolshevik seizure of power in the autumn of that year, referred to in Russia as the "October Revolution."

would be able to consolidate their hold on the country.

**Post-Armistice Objectives of Soviet Foreign Policy.** In these circumstances, two objectives now became dominant in Soviet foreign policy. The first was to produce a second, and genuinely Soviet, revolution in Germany, which could give the decisive impulse to European revolution generally. The second, conceived as a temporary expedient to preserve Bolshevik power in Russia during the interval until the European revolution might occur, was to persuade the western Allies (a) to remove their troops from Russia and (b) to establish with the Soviet regime such official relations as would assure against a renewal of intervention and would make possible a modicum of renewed trade and perhaps of economic assistance from western countries. The accumulative economic dislocations of foreign war, revolution, and civil war were by this time causing acute distress and chaos in Russian economic life; and it was becoming increasingly apparent that without assistance from the industrial countries of the West, the Russian economy was hardly to be restored.

**Early Hopes for Revolution in Europe.** The German revolution of November 1918 had brought into power there a moderate-socialist regime. Hopes were initially entertained in Moscow that this regime would evolve rapidly (following the pattern of the Russian Provisional Government) in the direction of a Soviet form of government, and would provide for Moscow an escape from the isolation and danger in which it still found itself. It soon became clear, however, that the new German government (a) was more concerned to propitiate the western victors than to establish close relations with the Russian communists and (b) was prepared, if necessary, to ally itself with the conservative force of the German army in order to preserve order in the face of the restless violence of groups at the extreme right and extreme left of the political spectrum. These last included even the extreme left-wing faction called the Spartacists, headed by Karl Liebknecht and Rosa Luxembourg, which was closest to Lenin in its views, which had his political blessing, and which was generally regarded as the German counterpart of the Bolsheviki. To these sources of conflict between Moscow and the new German government there were added many delays and differences in connection with the withdrawal of German troops from Russian territory.

Faced with these difficulties in the relationship with the new German regime, and always mindful of the supreme importance of the German workers for the cause of world revolution, the Soviet leaders lost no time in settling on a policy of promoting, by every means at their disposal, a second and "truly socialist" German revolution, which would overthrow the moderate-socialists and open the way to a German Soviet republic under Spartacist leadership. One of the leading Bolsheviki, Karl Radek, was despatched to Germany soon after the armistice, to lend what assistance he could, on behalf of the Soviet government, to the further revolutionary process in Germany. Within a few weeks after the German collapse, the Spartacists split off from the Social-Democratic Party and set themselves up as a German Communist Party.

Soviet hopes for an early European revolution were encouraged, in the winter of 1918-1919, by the emergence for brief periods of left-wing socialist regimes in Bavaria and Hungary. Contrary to popular impression, the establishment of these regimes was not the result of direct Soviet manipulation. It was only in Hungary, and then only in the later stages of the effort, that Soviet influence was predominant.[2] Both regimes were suppressed within a period of weeks. But they naturally caused, while they lasted, great and hopeful excitement in communist circles in Moscow, just as they caused alarm in western Europe.

On the level of German national politics, however, Soviet hopes for a communist revolution met almost at once with a series of grievous setbacks. In January 1919 a poorly organized and confused attempt by the communists to seize power in Berlin failed of its purpose, provoked counteraction on the part of the government,

[2] It is interesting to recall, in the light of the Soviet action in Hungary in 1956, that on this occasion in 1919 the Soviet government actually contemplated sending troops to assist the Hungarian revolution and at one time even issued orders (soon canceled) for their despatch. It is also interesting to note, in this connection, the Russian military intervention in Hungary, for purely political reasons, in 1849.

and resulted in the communists being deprived over a period of some months of all possibility for serious political action. In the course of these events, Liebknecht and Luxembourg were brutally murdered by right-wing extremists, forerunners of the Nazis. Radek was arrested and subjected to an imprisonment which lasted nearly a year. Although at first severely handled, he was later accorded remarkably lenient and indulgent treatment at the hands of his German jailers. This appears to have been the result of the influence of the German army leaders. Even at that early date some of the senior German officers, under Radek's encouragement, had begun to evince an interest in better relations with Moscow as a possible means of escape from the isolation and helplessness inflicted on Germany by the victorious European Allies. They realized that Radek might eventually become a useful intermediary in the pursuit of such a policy.

**The Founding of the Comintern.** In addition to these reverses, a new danger loomed for Lenin, in the winter of 1918-1919, in the prospect of the early revival, under moderate-socialist leadership, of the so-called Second International. This was an association of socialist parties of the world. Its operation had been disrupted for some years by the stresses and antagonisms of the war. Plainly, if the International should be restored under noncommunist leadership, this would not only strengthen the hands of the moderate-socialist government in Germany but it would confirm and formalize control by the moderates of the world socialist movement, damaging the prospects for a European communist revolution and leaving Lenin and his radical-socialist followers in a position of isolation even within the socialist sector of international life. Capitalizing, therefore, on the prestige which the Russian communists had gained through their successful seizure of power in Russia, Lenin hastened to organize in Moscow the first and founding congress of a rival organization, to be called the Third or "Communist" International (usually shortened to "Comintern"). By this device, he hoped to draw under his leadership initially, at least, the left-wing, and eventually the entire body, of the world socialist movement.

Since there was little contact at that time between Russia and other countries, and since time did not permit the accrediting and despatching of representatives of the left-wing factions abroad, this founding "congress" of the Comintern was largely a *pro forma* gathering, made up primarily of representatives of the Bolsheviki themselves and of the socialist parties of the former minority peoples of the Russian Empire, together with a few foreign socialists who happened to be in Russia at the time. But there was one representative from the German Communist Party. In view of the importance of the German socialist movement, this German delegate rated as the most important of the tiny handful of bona fide foreign delegates. He was actually under instructions not to approve the establishment of a Third, or "Communist," International, and abstained on the crucial vote, thus casting a considerable doubt on the political legitimacy of the action. Nevertheless, the decision was carried through, and the organization was formally established. (*See Document No. 5.*) It provided Lenin with the rudiments of an international vehicle through which his influence could now be regularly manifested in the international workers' movement. Eventually the Comintern gained strength and came to command the loyalty, and even obedience, of a sizable left-wing minority among the European labor movement. It remained, however, under strictest domination of the Russian communists, and soon became primarily a vehicle for the policies of the Soviet leaders rather than a political instrument and mouthpiece of international communist sentiment.

**Relations with the Allies.** While these things were happening on the world revolutionary front, efforts were also put forward to regularize relations with the Allies. The presence of the Allied forces in Russia still represented, of course, a serious danger and embarrassment to the new regime. To the expeditions in Siberia and North Russia, there had now been added (in December 1918) a French expedition, sent via the Black Sea to Odessa and its environs. The British, furthermore, had made minor incursions, with expeditions consisting of a few British officers and handfuls of native troops, from Persia northwards to both sides of the Caspian Sea. During the final weeks of 1918 and just after the turn of the year, the Soviet government made a whole series of approaches to the Allied governments through various channels, appealing for talks with a view to the termination of the intervention and the normalization of relations.

But there was no unity at that time among the Allied chanceries as to what ought to be done about Russia. Instead of replying to these approaches the Allies, understandably, left the problem for discussion by the senior statesmen, who were about to convene (mid-January 1919) for the Paris Peace Conference.

At the Peace Conference the Allied leaders made a series of efforts, largely futile, to compose the raging differences, not only among the various Allied governments but also within their own respective entourages, on policy toward Russia. On three occasions, as a result of these efforts, exchanges of one sort or another occurred between the senior statesmen at the Peace Conference and the Soviet government. In these exchanges, the Soviet government offered relatively far-reaching concessions (including even an amnesty to their opponents in the civil war) which the Allies would have been well advised to accept. (*See Document No. 6.*) But in no case could agreement be reached. The influence of the exiled anti-Bolshevik Russian factions in the corridors of the Peace Conference, and the stubborn hostility of the French, in particular, to any arrangement that implied acceptance of the Soviet regime, were sufficient to assure that any terms to which the Allies could agree were bound to appear to the Soviet leaders as ones that would deprive them of their almost certain victory in the civil war.[3]

As the Peace Conference reached its conclusion in the late spring of 1919, there was thus not only no agreement between the Allied governments and the Bolsheviki about the termination of the intervention, but the Allied

[3] This was particularly true of the proposals made, in May 1919, by the senior Allied statesmen at the Conference, at the instance of Herbert Hoover in his capacity as Allied Food Administrator. These proposals envisaged the distribution of Allied food in Russia within the framework of a general cease-fire. The terms on which this offer was made would unquestionably, if accepted, have made it most difficult for the Soviet regime to remain in power.

statesmen, to make matters worse, had begun to commit themselves increasingly to the fortunes of the anticommunist regime which, under the titular leadership of Admiral A. V. Kolchak, had emerged in the wake of the Czech uprising as the dominant power in Siberia. Misleading and out-of-date reports received in Paris in April and May 1919 of military successes Kolchak was supposed to have had, contributed greatly to this drift of Allied policy.

**The Termination of the Intervention.** Scarcely had the Peace Conference ended than Kolchak's fortunes began the disastrous decline which was to lead within the space of a few months to the crushing of his regime and to his own capture and execution. This sealed the fate of the intervention. One after another, the various Allied expeditions were withdrawn—not as a result of any agreement with the Soviet government nor because they had suffered any serious military defeat, but simply because they had proved inadequate to their purpose and because their maintenance had become burdensome to their respective governments. In the North, and in the Odessa area, the Allied forces left in the course of 1919. The American troops in Siberia, who had been kept there after the armistice primarily to act as a restraint on the Japanese, were withdrawn in the spring of 1920. The European Allies, in late 1919 and early 1920, continued to give material support to Generals Denikin and Wrangel, who were opposing Soviet authority in the South. But by the latter part of 1920 these undertakings, too, had been successfully repressed by the Bolsheviki. With their defeat, the episode of the Allied intervention was substantially at an end, except for the fact that the Japanese continued until 1925 to occupy the northern part of the island of Sakhalin.

Viewed as a whole, the Allied intervention of 1918-1920 did not resemble in any way the major concerted effort to overthrow the Soviet government which Soviet historiography today depicts it as having been. It consisted merely of a series of confused and uncoordinated military efforts, almost negligible in scale, lacking in any central plan, and having their initial origins, for the most part, in the necessities of the war with Germany. More serious damage was probably done to the Soviet government by the support given by the Allies to the Russian Whites in supplies and munitions than was done by the Allied expeditions themselves. However, the intervention, coinciding as it did with the Russian civil war, came as a profound shock to the Soviet leaders, confirming them in many of their ideological prejudices, convincing them of the inalterable hostility of the capitalist world, providing an excellent excuse, destined to be employed through decades to come, for the maintenance of the severe dictatorship within Russia.

**The Russian-Polish War of 1920.** There remained to be experienced in the way of intervention only the curious and dramatic events of the Polish-Russian war of 1920. This conflict originated from a most unwise attempt by the Poles to take advantage of Russia's weakness and to effect a major incursion into the Ukraine in the winter and spring of 1920. A Soviet counterattack in the north, launched in early summer, carried Soviet forces in a series of rapid advances to the gates of Warsaw. For a time, in midsummer, the fall of the city seemed certain. This development occasioned great excitement in Moscow, where the delegates to the Second Congress of the Third International, then in session, followed with wild enthusiasm the progress of the Soviet forces. In western Europe the news of the Soviet advance occasioned a corresponding alarm in conservative circles. People had visions of Soviet troops arriving at the German frontiers, bringing revolution to Germany, and making common cause with the resentful and vengeful Germans. A high-powered Allied mission, including as its senior military representative the French General Maxime Weygand, was at once despatched to Poland by the Allied governments. Shortly after its arrival the Poles, in a dramatic reversal of military fortunes, administered to the Soviet forces before Warsaw a severe and decisive defeat, still referred to as the "miracle of Warsaw." [4] The Soviet

[4] Commonly attributed to Weygand's genius, this victory was actually not his doing. The Allied mission had indeed done useful work in stiffening the administrative procedures of the Polish forces; but the strategic concept underlying the Polish action belonged unquestionably to the Polish President, Marshal Pilsudski. There is no

forces were then obliged to conduct a retirement no less hasty than their previous advance.

As a result of this turn of events, the war ended in a compromise peace, the territorial provisions of which were generally favorable to Poland.

**Continued Failure of the Revolutionary Effort in Germany.** While the intervention was being liquidated and the conflict with Poland pursued to its conclusion, there was no abatement of the Soviet effort to promote a communist revolution in Germany. But misfortune continued to dog the path of the German communists. In March 1920, irregular military units under fascist leadership launched an attack on Berlin, generally referred to as the Kapp Putsch, with a view to unseating the government and seizing power. The German workers, acting under moderate-socialist trade union leadership, successfully repulsed this action by means of a general strike. The communists, reluctant to support any action which was not under their own leadership and for which they could not get the bulk of the political credit, yet fearful to remain completely on the outside in the event the action should prove successful, played a hesitant, contradictory, and somewhat ludicrous role in the whole affair. They thereby forfeited once more an important measure of political prestige.

In a series of intricate and confused dealings with the various radical-socialist factions of Germany, Moscow continued to exert its influence, throughout the remaining months of 1920 and the winter of 1920-1921, with a view to consolidating the badly torn communist element in Germany, and to helping it recoup its prestige and win sufficient support to undertake a successful revolutionary action. These pressures reached their culmination in March 1921, when the German communists, under Soviet encouragement and in the face of serious misgivings on the part of a number of their own leaders, launched the

question but that the Polish success was partly due to a major failure of coordination of the Soviet military effort in Poland: a matter in which Stalin was personally involved and which led to lasting bitterness between him and the Soviet commander of the northern group of forces in Poland, General Tukhachevski.

second of the three major efforts they made in the immediate postwar years to seize power.[5] An insurrection was first proclaimed against the government. When this met with meager and inadequate response, the communists attempted to mount a general strike, as the moderate-socialists had done so successfully the year before. This, too, failed miserably. The result was a disastrous political reverse for the communists, who lost roughly one-half of their 350,000 members as a result of it.

**The Kronstadt Uprising.** The effects of the failure of the March 1921 action in Germany were rendered doubly painful for the Soviet leaders by the fact that this episode coincided closely in time with the uprising against the Soviet government of the disaffected sailors at the Kronstadt naval base. This uprising, which the government was forced to suppress by brutal and bloody military action, constituted a shocking revelation of the degree to which the government had lost the confidence of some of those very elements who had initially comprised the core of its popular support. Coming simultaneously with peasant revolts in the Kuban and Tambov regions, it was a severe blow to the internal and external prestige of the regime.

**The New Economic Policy.** The embarrassment of the Soviet leaders was further compounded, just at this time, by the fact that the Russian economy had by now deteriorated to a dangerous and almost intolerable degree. By the spring of 1921, the situation had become so serious that Lenin was obliged to promulgate his so-called "New Economic Policy" (N.E.P.), involving major, if temporary, concessions to private enterprise. This was justified to the supporters of the regime on the grounds that it was an unavoidable compromise with the class enemy: a tactical retreat designed to make possible future further advance.

**The 1921 Turning Point.** Plainly, these events of the winter and spring of 1921 marked, in their entirety, an important turning point in Soviet foreign relations. In two important respects the early calculations of the Soviet leaders had been confounded. Revolution, in Mos-

[5] The first was the action in January 1919, mentioned above. The third was the action undertaken in the autumn of 1923 (see Chapter 4).

cow's sense, had *not* occurred in any of the great countries of Europe. There was no reason to suppose that it would occur at any early date. On the other hand, the Soviet state had *not* collapsed, nor had it been overthrown, as a result of the failure of world revolution to mature. (*See Document No. 7.*) The initial military challenge by which it had been faced, internally and externally, had now—with the termination of the Polish war—been survived. For the first time since the early spring of 1918 the Soviet government was relieved of the necessity of waging war. But it was now threatened by the appalling state of the Russian economy. This situation was further aggravated during the course of 1921 by a catastrophic drought in some of the main grain-growing regions. In these circumstances, the cause of world revolution naturally receded into the background as an immediate objective of Soviet policy, though it remained as a long-term goal. The development of economic and political relations with the leading capitalist governments, on the other hand, assumed new importance. (*See Document No. 8.*)

Heretofore, believing that the "breathing-space" would soon be terminated either by world revolution or by the suppression of Soviet power at the hands of the international bourgeoisie, the Soviet leaders had regarded the discussion of possible trade with the West primarily as a means of playing the capitalist nations off against each other and dissuading them from launching a real attack on Russia. Now, as world revolution continued to fail to arrive and as the reconstruction of the Russian economy became a matter of urgent necessity, the possibility of restoring economic relations with the West became a dominant consideration in Soviet policy.

**The Need for Trade, Credits, and Recognition.** There were three things that the Soviet government needed from the West to assure its own success at home: trade, credits, and recognition.

Russia urgently needed extensive imports of capital goods from the West. She had certain accumulations of raw material, actual or possible, which could be used to pay for imports on a barter basis. But these export possibilities were insufficient. If imports were to be assured in adequate amounts, credits would also be needed.

An outstanding difficulty was present, here, in the fact that the Soviet government, shortly after its accession to power, had disclaimed all responsibility for the foreign debts of previous Russian regimes as well as any obligation to reimburse the foreign owners of property in Russia which had been nationalized in the process of the revolution. Since the Russian government had been, on the eve of the revolution, the greatest of international debtors, and since foreign investment in Russia was heavy, the claims of the outside world against the Soviet government under these headings were very substantial ones, totaling something like 20 billion dollars in today's currency.

The Soviet leaders considered that to acknowledge any general responsibility to meet these claims would be to place themselves in a state of permanent vassalage to the western capitalists. At no time did they ever consider assuming such an obligation in principle. But they were prepared, as a *quid pro quo* for the extension of new credits from the West, to make token payments, in the form of extra interest on new credits, which could be used by the recipient governments to liquidate at least a small portion of the old indebtedness. They hoped in this way to overcome some of the hesitations on the western side.

The difficulties in the way of obtaining long-term credits from the West were increased, obviously, by lack of diplomatic recognition on the part of the western governments. If western financiers were unwilling to contemplate the granting of credit to a government which had repudiated the debts of its predecessors, they would plainly be all the more disinclined to do this so long as the government in question was one which their own governments had not recognized. The quest for diplomatic recognition by the western governments therefore became a concomitant of the Soviet drive for trade and credits. It might well be asked what reason the Soviet leaders had to suppose that the western governments and financiers would be willing to lend their collaboration for the economic strengthening of a political entity whose ultimate purpose, still frequently and openly avowed, was to destroy them. The answer given to this question in Moscow was that western capitalism was so blind in its greed, so compulsively addicted to the quest for immediate profit, so wracked by internal rivalries and differences (in communist parlance, "contradictions"), that it could easily be brought to trade with its enemies, if profit were involved. Capitalism was, in the Marxist view, the helpless victim, not the master, of the developing social forces on which it was borne; it had no control over its own fate; it could thus be brought "to dig its own grave." (*See Document No. 8.*)

It may be noted, in passing, that this cynical analysis on the part of the Soviet leadership proved, in the point at issue, to be *in principle* correct. Nowhere in the West were businessmen deterred from seeking trade with the Soviet government by the reflection that such trade would strengthen the hands of men whose lives were dedicated to the achievement of a world order in which there would be no private business at all. But the Soviet leaders erred in their estimation of the terms on which western businessmen would insist. Believing capitalism to be in a desperate position, they overestimated the importance of the Soviet market for foreign firms, and underestimated the caution such firms would show in the development of dealings with so undependable a partner as the Soviet Foreign Trade Monopoly.

**The Policy of Concessions.** One particular possibility which occupied a considerable place in Soviet thinking about economic relations with the capitalist world in the early twenties was that of granting concessions to capitalist firms for the exploitation of raw materials on Soviet territory, in return for the supply of capital equipment. A decree establishing the procedures whereby this might be done was issued by the Soviet government on November 23, 1920. Such fruit as it bore was destined to be forthcoming only at a later date, and to remain within very modest dimensions. But in the autumn of 1920 this idea interested Lenin intensely and was the subject of a good deal of public discussion.

That the contemplated concessions to foreign capitalists were expected to produce some economic advantage to the Soviet state cannot be denied; but it is also clear that the main uses of this device, in Lenin's view, were political. His mind was at that time still preoccupied with the conviction that the capitalist governments would wish at some point to resume the military intervention against the Soviet state. The granting of concessions to individual foreign entrepreneurs was seen in Moscow primarily as a device for enlisting the personal interest of western capitalists in the preservation of decent relations between their respective countries and Moscow. It was also hoped that such arrangements would fan the flames of commercial rivalry and tension between various foreign countries, particularly between the United States and Japan, but also between the United States and the great powers of Europe.

**Revival of Trade and Contacts with Britain.** The desire of the Soviet leaders for the formal regularization of relations with the western countries met with a growing, though hesitant and divided, response in the Allied countries. Powerful anti-Soviet feelings continued to be manifested, particularly in France. But there were also many who were coming to feel that if the Soviet government was not to be destroyed, then an effort must be made to find some sort of *modus vivendi* with it, under which commercial exchanges, at least, could be resumed.

Efforts toward at least a limited regularization of relations with the Soviet Union were put in hand by western circles even before the termination of the civil war. On January 16, 1920, largely under the influence of the British Prime Minister, David Lloyd George (who had often been skeptical, like Wilson, of the wisdom of the intervention), the Allied Supreme Council removed the blockade against Russia and approved, in principle, negotiations looking forward to a renewed exchange of goods between Russia and the Allied countries. This left the individual Allied governments free to shape their own policies toward Russia. Shortly thereafter British and Soviet representatives met, for the first time, in Copenhagen, and arrived (on February 11) at an agreement for the exchange of prisoners-of-war. On May 17, 1920 a group of Soviet trade negotiators, headed by Leonid Krassin, arrived in London, and began talks looking to the conclusion of a trade agreement between the two countries.

The negotiations were prolonged. They met at every point with bitter opposition in conservative circles in Britain. They suffered long interruption as a result of the insistence of the British government on coupling the issues of the Russian-Polish war of 1920 with the question of the resumption of trade. There were serious inhibitions to be overcome on both sides. But on March 16, 1921, at approximately the same time as the Kronstadt uprising and the failure of the communist action in Germany, an agreement was finally signed in London.

This was a provisional arrangement, designed to operate only pending the conclusion of a formal and general treaty of peace. It provided for immediate resumption of trade negotiations but not for normal diplomatic intercourse. It signified *de facto*, but not as yet *de jure*, recognition of the Soviet government by Great Britain. It contained a clause barring "official propaganda" by either party against the institutions of the other. The difficult question of debts and claims was left for treatment in the later permanent settlement. As a result of the agreement, unofficial representatives were exchanged between the two countries.

**The Famine.** Foreign assistance in the restoration of the Soviet economy was first received in a major way in connection with the severe famine by which the Soviet Union was visited in the years 1921 and 1922. The causes of this disaster lay partly in the drought of the 1921 season but also extensively in the unfortunate effects of the experimentation the Soviet government had conducted with the agricultural system of the country. By midsummer 1921 the situation was so appalling that it was finally recognized as necessary to make an appeal to the outside world for famine relief. The Party leaders, reluctant to do this in their own name, caused it to be done through the mouth of the writer Maxim Gorky. (*See Document No. 9.*) A number of foreign organizations responded to this appeal. Of these the most important, in the scale of its resources and of its operations in Russia, was the American Relief Administration, directed by Herbert Hoover. Using funds provided partly by the Soviet government itself, partly by private organizations in the United States, and mainly by the United States government, the ARA, as it was called, moved in with great vigor and promptness to alleviate the effects of the famine. By August 1922, a staff of 200 Americans was working in Russia, directing the operation of over 18,000 feeding stations, at which more than 4,000,000 children and 6,000,000 adults were fed. All in all, 788,000 tons of food were imported and distributed by ARA. Medical assistance was also provided on a massive scale. It is soberly estimated that ARA's effort alone saved 11,000,000 lives, of which at least a third were those of children and young people.

Although the Soviet leaders had themselves invited this aid, it was at once apparent that their principal concern, with respect to ARA's operations, was to see that the relief organization did not become a focal point for political opposition among the Russian population. To this end it made intensive efforts to gain full disciplinary power over ARA's 200,000 Russian employees and control over the handling and distribution of the food. ARA had no choice, in the interests of the program, but to resist these efforts.

When ARA finally terminated its program, appreciation for the services of the Americans was formally expressed by the Soviet government. In later years, however, the Soviet view of ARA's work underwent a change. ARA is now generally portrayed by Soviet historians as an effort by the American capitalists to penetrate Russia and to overthrow the Soviet regime. It is sometimes admitted that ARA "gave a certain help to the starving." [6]

# — 4 —

# RAPALLO AND ITS AFTERMATH

**The Resumption of Official Contacts with Germany.** The success of the effort of the Soviet government to win trade, credits, and recognition from the western governments turned out, as will shortly be seen, to revolve largely around the position of the German govern-

[6] I. I. Mints, Editor, *Sovyetskaya Rossiya i kapitalisticheskii mir v 1917-1923 gg.* (Soviet Russia and the Capitalist World, 1917-1923), Moscow, 1957, p. 497.

ment. For this reason, it now becomes necessary to go back to the break of 1918, and to trace the process by which official contacts were resumed between the Soviet and German governments.

As the world war came to an end, mutual repatriation of German and Russian prisoners-of-war was, for various reasons, a matter of urgent necessity to the German government. Hindered for some time by Allied restrictions,[1] the German government received only in late 1919 permission from the Allied governments to proceed with arrangements for repatriation. Negotiations were at once put in hand, and an agreement was signed on April 19, 1920, prescribing the modalities of this operation.[2] This agreement provided for the stationing in the respective capitals of official "prisoner-of-war" representatives.

Beyond this, initially, the responsible German political leaders were reluctant to go in the development of formal relations with Moscow. However, the severe rebuff administered to German hopes by the Allies with respect to reparations and military controls, at the Spa Conference in midsummer 1920, caused a considerable shift of influential opinion in Germany. This tendency was strengthened by the effect of the approach of the Red Army to the German border that same summer, in the course of the Russian-Polish War. This last brought home to many Germans the possibilities of a development of German-Soviet relations as an alternative to a helpless and hopeless acceptance of the strictures of the Versailles Treaty. Throughout the ensuing years, in general, it may be said that the prospering of German-Soviet relations, or at least the effort put forward on the German side to cause them to prosper, remained a function of the degree of discouragement and frustration brought to the Germans, at any given moment, by the policies of the British and the French. It was in the summer of 1920 that this process began.

[1] The French had a fatuous idea of using Russian war prisoners in Germany to support the intervention, and for some time they refused to permit the Germans to make any move toward exchange of these prisoners.

[2] It appears to have been chance, rather than design, which caused this agreement to follow so closely after the similar British agreement, signed February 12, 1920.

The alarm caused in western Europe by the initial Russian success in the war against Poland made a deep impression on Lenin. With the exaggeration characteristic of much Soviet political thought, he easily persuaded himself that the Soviet Union had almost succeeded, by its military action in Poland, in destroying the entire "system" of Versailles. He was particularly intrigued to note the effect of the Polish war in inclining many German conservatives in favor of collaboration with Moscow. As time went on, he and his associates were to become increasingly aware of the ironic circumstances that in their relations with the German Left, where they had most hopefully and confidently looked for the salvation of their regime, they suffered only frustration; whereas in their relations with the German Right, toward whose members they bore nothing but loathing and contempt, possibilities arose for dealings and arrangements which could be, if not of vital importance, at least of considerable advantage to the Soviet state. (*See Document No. 10.*)

**German-Soviet Military Collaboration.** The improvement in German-Russian relations, beginning in the latter months of 1920, proceeded on two quite separate planes: the military and the political.

Aware of the growing interest of the German military leaders in developing relations with the Soviet Union, needing foreign help in the reconstruction of their own armaments industry, and shaken by the final reverses of the Russian-Polish War, the Soviet authorities put out hints to German military circles, in the autumn of 1920, that they would not be averse to exploring the possibilities of certain kinds of military collaboration. General Hans von Seeckt responded by sending first an officer to Russia, in January 1921, and later in the year a small military mission, to study and develop these possibilities. All this was done with greatest secrecy. Later in 1921, as the talks with the Russians proceeded favorably, institutional arrangements were set up within the German military establishment to handle and to conceal the respective operations.

Out of these beginnings developed the clandestine collaboration between the German Reichswehr and the

Soviet government which began, as a practical matter, in 1922 and which endured, with vicissitudes, for roughly a decade, until shortly after Hitler's accession to power. Because the real nature of this collaboration was carefully concealed, and only hints of it reached public attention, its importance and sinisterness have often been exaggerated. Its operation, actually, was marked from the outset by many misunderstandings, difficulties, and false starts. Much that was originally conceived had to be abandoned. The residue of positive achievement was such as to represent a marginal, but not insignificant, factor in the rearmament of both countries. The Russians obtained in this way some German technical assistance in the training of the Red Army in the use of modern weapons, and a modest degree of German collaboration in the reconstruction of their armaments industry. They also obtained the possibility of training a number of their higher officers in German military schools. Conversely, the arrangements made it possible for the Germans to train air force personnel and tank crews, on a limited scale, in Russia, thus evading the pertinent restrictions of the Versailles settlement. They were able to construct in Russia a few Junkers aircraft for the needs of this training program and for other purposes. They succeeded in procuring considerable quantities of ammunition from Russian plants built or restored with their technical assistance.

These arrangements, while usually (not always) pleasing to those on both sides who sought closer relations between the two countries, were not political in origin. They came with time to have, naturally, a certain political significance, in the sense that any abrupt disruption of them would have disturbed political relations. But they did not constitute an alliance, or a political compact of any sort. They owed their existence to the simple fact that they were momentarily useful to both parties. They were entered into by both parties in a spirit of *caveat emptor*, in full awareness of the wide divergence of political purpose that marked the positions of the two governments. Contemporary Soviet historiography tends to portray them as the products of Trotskyite treachery and to imply that they were conducted behind the backs of the responsible officials of the Party.[3] This is, of course, nonsense. It is preposterous to suppose, in the face of the nature of the Soviet political system and the facilities available to the Soviet leaders for knowing what went on in their own country, that activities of this sort by foreigners, including construction of an airplane plant in the Moscow suburb of Fili, could have proceeded without knowledge and approval of the Party leadership as a whole.

On the German side, the preparatory contacts leading to the military arrangements were initially concealed from most of the responsible officials of the political echelons of the German government, including even the President and Foreign Minister. This secrecy could not be observed indefinitely. By the end of 1922, most of the senior political officials had become personally aware that arrangements of this nature existed. The details continued, however, to be closely held on the military side; and the political echelons of the government, outside the Minister of Finance, whose collaboration was essential, avoided taking official cognizance of the arrangements.

**The Development of German-Soviet Political Relations.** The trend of German opinion toward closer relations with Russia, after late 1920, caused a sharp division of views in the higher civilian echelons of the German government. The President, Friedrich Ebert, and the successive foreign ministers, remained generally averse to any development of these relations going beyond the practice, at the given moment, of the leading Allied powers. However, a small group of influential figures, including the head of the Russian bureau in the Foreign

[3] This thesis is based, presumably, on the fact of Trotsky's position as Commissar for War at the time they were concluded, and of Karl Radek's role as an intermediary. Radek appeared, in 1937, among the defendants in one of the three great purge trials, where he confessed extravagantly to charges of opposition activity on behalf of the Trotskyites. Here, as in most cases of this nature, the confession was as untrustworthy as the indictment; but in view of the failure of the Party leadership to repudiate, as yet, *this* portion of Stalin's injustices, Radek is still stamped in Soviet historiography as having always been a Trotskyite.

Office, Baron Ago van Maltzan, the war-prisoner delegate at Moscow, Moritz Schlesinger, and the future chancellor, Josef Wirth, were deeply convinced of the need for developing the political relationship with the Russians. These men, and others who favored closer relations with Russia, were often referred to as the "Easterners." They pressed with vigor and skill the improvement of German-Soviet relations. Schlesinger, in the winter of 1921, negotiated with the Soviet government the text of an agreement on the basis of which the war-prisoner delegates would be replaced by official consular representatives (though not by ambassadors). This agreement, following the pattern of the Anglo-Soviet Trade Agreement, then still under negotiation, envisaged a resumption of commercial exchanges. The signing on March 12, 1921, of the British agreement removed one major obstacle to the final signature of the German-Soviet document. Yet the responsible heads of the German government, despite pressures from the "Easterners," hesitated to take the step of signing it. The matter remained suspended until the Allies, in early May 1921, made public the final formulation of their reparations bill against Germany—for a total of 132 billion gold marks. The German cabinet, being unwilling to accept this demand, resigned; but before leaving office it signed the agreement with the Soviet Union, as a last gesture of protest against the Allied action.

The new German cabinet took a quite different line, and dedicated itself politically to the effort to meet the Allied demands. This required a soft-pedaling of the relationship with Moscow. For some months Maltzan and the others were frustrated in their efforts to achieve any further development of Soviet-German relations. In the autumn of 1921, however, the announcement of the League of Nations decision on the partition of Upper Silesia, felt by the Germans to be unfair to their side, brought discredit on those who had staked their political fortunes on the effort to fulfill the French and British requirements. A change of policy occurred. The path was now cleared for further negotiations with Russia.

**The Genoa Conference.** In the meantime, the question of economic relations between Russia and the western countries had become widely linked, in public discussion throughout Europe, with the problems of reparations and of European reconstruction generally. The deplorable plight of the Russian economy, together with the announced changes in Soviet economic policy, encouraged people in the West to believe that the Soviet government might now be prepared to accept the participation of western capital on a massive scale in the rehabilitation of the Russian economy, as part of the general reconstruction of Europe. There was much talk at this time of the establishment of an international consortium to undertake both this reconstruction of Russia and the development of Russia's trade with Europe.

The Soviet leaders regarded these suggestions with alarm. They were made uneasy, in fact, by even the slightest suggestion of a united approach among the western powers to the problems of trade with Russia. They saw favorable possibilities for themselves in the resumption of trade exchanges only in the event that they could deal with the European countries individually, retaining the ability to play them off against one another.

In the winter of 1921-1922, Lloyd George (acting largely out of internal political motives) took the lead in promoting a general conference for the economic reconstruction of Europe, to be held at Genoa. Both Soviet Russia and Germany were to be invited. (Neither had previously been asked to attend any of the postwar international conferences.) A last-minute refusal by the French to permit reparations to be discussed left little for such a conference to deal with except the economic relations between the western countries and Russia. Plans for the gathering nevertheless went forward. It finally convened in early April 1922.

The idea of an international conference to deal with the re-establishment of economic exchanges and the establishment of a definite state of peace between Russia and the West was not, in itself, uncongenial to the Soviet government. The People's Commissar for Foreign Affairs, G. V. Chicherin, had in fact himself suggested something of the sort in a note addressed to the Allied powers on October 28, 1921. (*See Document No. 11.*) But the abundant discussion in western Europe, in the winter of 1920-1921, of various schemes for a consortium to deal with Russian reconstruction alarmed the

Soviet leaders. They came to have increasing misgivings about the conference, as proposed by Lloyd George. They accepted the invitation to Genoa; but they did so apprehensively. As the time for the conference neared, they applied their diplomatic resources intensively to the task of disrupting a possible united front of the capitalists against them. To this end, they endeavored to induce the Germans to commit themselves, in advance of the conference, to what would be in effect a separate treaty of peace with Russia.

In this effort they were aided not only by the eager collaboration of Maltzan and the other "Easterners" in the German government, who did not hesitate to begin discussion with Soviet representatives of the possible language of such an agreement before any formal authority for this had been obtained from their superiors in the German government, but also by German fear of the invocation of Article 116 of the Treaty of Versailles. The French, thinking that this might be useful to the prospects for collection of their prewar loans to Russia, had taken pains to have included in the Versailles Treaty a provision (Article 116) which held open the possibility of Russia's some day joining the western Allies in obtaining reparations from Germany. In doing this, the French were of course hoping that the Soviet government would soon be overthrown; and it was not the Soviet government but a possible noncommunist successor which they envisaged as the beneficiary of this clause.

The Soviet government, not recognizing the Versailles settlement, had never attempted to avail itself of this provision, and almost certainly did not intend to do so. But it was not averse to allowing the Germans to believe that the alternative to a special German-Russian peace settlement might be a general Russian agreement with the western Allied powers, involving the invocation of Article 116. With much diplomatic skill, Soviet diplomatists contrived to build up in the minds of the German statesmen, in the weeks prior to the opening of the Genoa Conference, the impression that this, in the event of the failure of the Germans to agree to a separate German-Soviet pact, would be a serious possibility.

On the eve of the opening of the Genoa Conference,

the Soviet delegation, headed personally by Chicherin, proceeded to Genoa via Berlin. Here they were successful in persuading the German government to join them in putting down on paper some of the provisions of a possible agreement providing for a mutual cancellation of claims and restoration of full diplomatic relations between the two governments. (On certain points, not treated in the official talks, language was threshed out privately in talks with Maltzan.) The two delegations thus went to Genoa with most of the language of a possible agreement already worked out. But the German government remained unwilling to sign any document in advance of the Conference.

The dramatic tale of what actually occurred at Genoa is too complex to be included in this narrative. (For Chicherin's opening speech, *see Document No. 12.*) Suffice it to say that the French and British representatives played handsomely into the hands of the Russian effort to split the Germans from the remainder of the European community.[4] Not only did they enter into private talks with the Soviet delegation, from which the Germans were carefully excluded, and then let it become known to the Germans that Article 116 was under discussion in these talks, but they carried the social ostracism of the German delegation to such a point that the Germans had no opportunity to obtain correct information as to what was really going on, or to inform the French and British (as they repeatedly tried to do) of their own anxieties. The Soviet representatives, who were in frequent contact with the German delegation, permitted the Germans to believe that there was real danger of a Soviet-British-French accord at the expense of the Germans, and hinted that the only way for the Germans to avert this would be the immediate signature of the Soviet-German pact.

Finally, on Easter Sunday, April 16, 1922, frightened by the growing impression that the alternative to a sep-

[4] Insofar as the British representation was concerned, this was strictly a nonprofessional conference. No senior Foreign Office official was included in the British delegation, which was headed personally by Lloyd George. The Foreign Secretary, Lord Curzon, was apprehensive from the start as to the result.

arate German-Soviet agreement would be the adherence of Russia to the group of those claiming reparations from Germany and, accordingly, the total political and economic isolation of Germany, the reluctant German Foreign Minister, Walter Rathenau, was induced by his associates to sign, at the headquarters of the Russian delegation in Rapallo, the German-Russian treaty which has lived in history as the Treaty of Rapallo.

This instrument, in itself, was relatively innocuous. (*See Document No. 13.*) It was not a treaty of alliance. It had no secret clauses or protocols. It consisted, basically, only of provision for the establishment of full diplomatic relations, for the mutual renunciation of claims (which relieved the Germans of the nightmare of Article 116, and meant, for the Russians, conversely, that there would be at least *one* great power which could not advance claims for the losses of its nationals in Russia), and for the extension of most-favored-nation treatment in commercial matters and in the treatment of nationals. Nevertheless, the news of its conclusion produced in London and Paris a shock of alarm and indignation, the effects of which were destined to be felt for years to come.

The conclusion of the Rapallo pact was a triumph of Soviet diplomacy. It established a useful precedent for diplomatic recognition by other great powers. It disrupted every possibility of a united front of the European powers in their economic dealings with Russia (and this at a moment of maximum Russian economic weakness). It detached Germany decisively and finally from the ranks of those pressing the Soviet government for payment of the debts of previous Russian governments and for compensation for the foreign property nationalized in the Russian revolution. (*See Document No. 14.*) To the Germans, too, it gave a flexibility in policy toward the victor states which had not previously been enjoyed.

**German-Soviet Relations After Rapallo.** The conclusion of the Rapallo pact led, of course, to the exchange of ambassadors. A senior Party official, N. Krestinski, was sent to Berlin. To Moscow in the autumn of 1922, the German government assigned Count Ulrich Brockdorff-Rantzau, a man of much ability and force of character, who had been the first Foreign Minister of the

German Republic, but had resigned in 1919 in protest against the Treaty of Versailles. Rantzau, though deeply embittered against the Allies and convinced that Germany would regain independence of action only by the development of relations with Russia, was a firm and consistent opponent of anything in the nature of a German-Russian alliance. He disapproved initially even of the clandestine military arrangements, and was adamant in refusing to encourage the Soviet government in any military ambitions. He established an excellent working arrangement with Chicherin, who was, like himself, of noble origin, and also entertained a strong bitterness toward Britain.

The first year of Rantzau's service in Moscow, from the autumn of 1922 to the autumn of 1923, was probably the heyday of the German-Russian relationship. The French occupation of the Ruhr left the Germans no choice but to play the Russian card. Under Rantzau's vigorous guidance, economic relations were rapidly developed. There was achieved an intimacy of diplomatic contact, as between the German Embassy and the Soviet Foreign Office, such as has probably never been enjoyed by any other noncommunist diplomatic mission to Moscow in time of peace.

**Chicherin's Difficulties.** Within the Party leadership, however, Chicherin was faced with opposition from two quarters in his efforts to develop relations with Germany. First, there were those who had by no means ceased to pursue the dream of world revolution, beginning with revolution in Germany, and whose intrigues with the German communists were a constant burden on the regular diplomatic relationship between the two countries. (*See Document No. 15.*) On the other hand, there was the rising star of Stalin, who was never loath to sacrifice to the uses of his personal domestic-political ambitions the good relations between the Soviet Union and western countries, and who always feared that any close relationship with a foreign government which was not created and maintained under his personal direction would turn out to be a threat to his personal position.

Lenin, it must be recalled, had his first stroke on May 26, 1922. His second occurred in December of that year. The winter of 1922-1923 was marked by a growing uneasiness on his part about Stalin. This culminated in the complete break of personal relations between the two men in March 1923—a crisis which was followed almost immediately by Lenin's third stroke, which wholly incapacitated him. This was the beginning of Stalin's gradual rise to a position of ascendancy.

**The "October" Action in Germany.** For some months of 1923, the Party leaders being largely preoccupied with internal-political matters, Chicherin had a relatively free hand. His efforts to cultivate good relations with Germany were aided by the French occupation of the Ruhr and the resulting tension in Germany's relations with the West. In late summer of 1923, however, the Germans abandoned the policy of passive resistance to the Ruhr occupation; and Gustav Stresemann, who at that time assumed the chancellorship, launched the program of improvement in the relations with the western Allied countries which was later to culminate in the Dawes Plan (for the collection of German reparations) and the Locarno Pact.

In Moscow, this trend of German policy was taken as a rebuff. Opinion in high Party circles moved, by consequence, in the direction of new efforts to promote a communist seizure of power in Germany. The German communists were once more encouraged by Moscow to institute armed action. In October 1923 they made the effort to comply, pushing their followers in various parts of Germany to the very brink of armed revolt. The action was easily suppressed by the Reichswehr. Communist prestige suffered a new and, this time, an irreparable blow.

The shock brought to German-Soviet relations by this development, in which the Russian hand was scarcely concealed, was severe. It constituted a serious setback to the policy Brockdorff-Rantzau was endeavoring to implement. The ensuing years of 1924 and 1925 were marked by a series of unpleasant incidents involving, on the German side, a police raid on the headquarters of the Soviet Trade Delegation and, on the Russian side, the "framing" of several German citizens and officials for propaganda purposes, in what was to become later the characteristic Stalin manner. In both these instances, the actions were taken by the internal authorities, over the heads of the respective foreign offices. By the patient efforts of Chicherin and Rantzau, the incidents were all eventually composed. But the intimacy of 1923 was never entirely restored.

**Anglo-Soviet Relations.** The conclusion of the Anglo-Soviet Trade Agreement of March 16, 1921, did not mark any great improvement in the general relations between the two countries. The months following its conclusion saw the beginning of a pattern of friction, centering around the question of anti-British communist propaganda (especially in the Middle East) which was to agitate Anglo-Soviet relations with monotonous regularity over the coming years. Here, the issue was often badly muddled. It was true that the Soviet leaders continued to conduct, in their capacity as officials of the Communist Party, anti-British propaganda which they had obligated themselves by the Trade Agreement, in their capacity as members of the Soviet government, not to conduct. To this extent, British grievances were justified. The British government, on the other hand, often relied for its information about these violations on White Russian circles who were only too glad to provide false proof where real proof was lacking. In the resulting acrid exchanges both sides tended to be at times right and at times wrong.

**Continued Negotiations over Debts and Claims.** In addition to this friction about propaganda, the major impediment to a regularization of Anglo-Soviet relations in this early period continued to be the thorny subject of debts and claims. The conclusion of the Rapallo Pact caused the French and British to exclude the Germans from further participation in the Genoa Conference; but the negotiations continued, first at Genoa and then in a later conference (June 15-July 20, 1922) at The Hague. They soon narrowed down to the question of the readiness of the Soviet government to meet the demands of the Allied governments in the field of debts and claims. Agreement would probably have been possible on the problem of the debts of former Russian governments; but the question of compensation for the foreign property nationalized in the course of the revolution proved insoluble. Here, the western governments were subject to pressures from powerful private firms whose interests were involved. None of the governments felt able to enter into an agreement which would undermine these interests.

After the breakdown of these various negotiations, talks continued between individual firms in the West and the Soviet government. Of these the most important were the talks conducted by the Russian-Asiatic Consolidated Company, Limited, of England. They led to the initialing in the autumn of 1922 of a separate agreement settling the claims of this company against the Soviet government, and providing for its further activity in Russia. At the last minute, however, this agreement, too, fell through. Lenin vetoed its ratification, calculating correctly that the Soviet government could probably win recognition and credits on a wide scale in the end, without making this sacrifice.

**The Lausanne Conference.** A special pungency was lent to these differences by the fact that British policy was conducted from 1917 to the end of 1923 by Lord Curzon, whose diplomatic skill and power of expression was such that he was able to carry his side of these differences with peculiar effectiveness. A major episode in Curzon's encounter with Soviet diplomacy was the conference at Lausanne, held in the winter and spring of 1922-1923, to frame a definitive treaty of peace between the Allies and the new nationalist regime of Kemal Pasha in Turkey. Soviet Russia was invited, as a littoral power of the Black Sea, to participate, but only in those sessions of the conference which dealt with the question of the regime of the Straits—a limitation against which the Soviet government vigorously protested.

The Soviet leaders had taken, from the start, a favorable attitude toward the new regime in Turkey. They approved particularly of its stout resistance to the continuation of the special privileges which the great powers had theretofore enjoyed in that country. This benevolence of attitude toward the Turks was, in fact, a forerunner of the tolerance which Moscow was to show on so much wider a scale in later decades for nationalist regimes in non-European countries whenever these latter were animated by anti-European sentiments and policies.

The Soviet delegation, headed by Chicherin, came to Lausanne, accordingly, with two main purposes. The first was to achieve maximum restriction of the right of foreign war vessels to enter the Black Sea. The other was to exploit the occasion to appear as the friends and protectors of the Turks, and, with them, of all smaller and weaker peoples, against the encroachments of the great capitalist powers. The official position taken by the Soviet delegation in the negotiations was one that favored closing of the Straits to the warships of outside powers, urged fortification of the Straits by the Turks, as a manifestation of their untrammeled sovereignty, and advocated the exclusion of all but the littoral powers of the Black Sea from any future participation in the discussion of problems relating to the Straits.

This program could not be realized at the conference. It did not command full agreement even among the littoral powers. Curzon, who headed the British delegation in person and who chaired the key committee of the conference, pressed his cause vigorously and with great skill. The Turks, who had previously shown sympathy with the Russian position, abandoned the Russians at the crucial moment. Curzon's proposals, diametrically opposed to those of Chicherin, became the basis of the decisions of the conference. These decisions called for demilitarization of the Straits. They left open, with minor restrictions, the right of passage for the warships of outside powers.

The Soviet attitude toward the regime of the Straits that flowed from the Lausanne Treaty was an unhappy and ambivalent one. The Soviet government signed the resulting Straits Convention, but failed to ratify it. Nevertheless it continued over a period of some years to observe the Convention to the extent of providing the Mixed Commission, set up to supervise the new regime of the Straits, with information on the strength of its own naval forces in the Black Sea, as the Convention provided.

**The Curzon Ultimatum.** During the latter phases of the Lausanne Conference, at a time when Curzon himself had returned to his desk at the Foreign Office, he addressed to the Soviet government (May 2, 1923) a memorandum reviewing the entire previous course of Anglo-Soviet relations, complaining particularly about the anti-British propaganda in the Middle East, and threatening to denounce the Trade Agreement of 1921 if satisfaction was not given. For a time, the two governments seemed on the edge of a break. But the Soviet government, particularly anxious at that moment not to prejudice the possibilities of full diplomatic recognition, adopted what—for Soviet usage—was a conciliatory tone in its reply (drafted, actually, by Trotsky) and contrived, without yielding anything in principle, to prolong the correspondence in such a way as to forestall the threatening action.

# — 5 —

# RECOGNITION AND THE PROBLEM OF EUROPEAN SECURITY

**Lenin's Death.** On January 21, 1924, Lenin died, after a long illness. For two years preceding his death, he had been able to exert influence only in limited degree on the conduct of official affairs. Nevertheless, the policies followed had been, in the main, those which he had originally approved. Here, as in domestic affairs, his passing marked a momentous, but not a sharp, turning point.

**Stalin's Qualities Compared to Lenin's.** Lenin's moral and intellectual ascendancy within the Russian communist movement was such that never, except briefly in the Brest-Litovsk crisis, was his authority seriously questioned. He was a man of compelling brilliance and originality—an intellectual by breeding and inclination. His pre-1917 experience lay largely with that portion of the revolutionary movement which had spent long periods of exile abroad. He knew the languages and traditions of the main European peoples. He felt fully at home among foreign socialist colleagues. Never for a moment did he fear or hesitate to take personal part in the debates and discussions of the world socialist movement. He considered himself, with good reason, fully qualified to hold his ground in this form of competition.

Stalin, who in the years following Lenin's death gradually consolidated his position as the successor, was a different sort of person. He was not endowed with brilliant or creative intellectual gifts. His genius lay in the field of organization, not of thought. He had spent his prerevolutionary past as a local party worker in Russia, largely in the underground. His experience of the outside world was negligible. Although he later compelled his entourage to do elaborate outward deference to his alleged powers as a theoretician, he was well aware of his own lack of originality, and knew that his thoughts never commanded respect for their own sake.

Stalin was ill at ease among foreigners, and uncomfortable in his personal relationship to the international side of the communist movement. His nightmare, throughout the period of his rule, was isolation and repudiation within the movement itself by people better educated and more cosmopolitan than himself. Conscious of his lack of Lenin's moral ascendancy within the movement, he was well aware of the danger of what is today called Titoism: of the possibility, that is, that the leaders of a foreign communist party, particularly one which was successful in seizing power by its own resources, would not be likely to recognize his authority, and might therefore become a source of inspiration and encouragement to the opposition within Russia. He never ceased, accordingly, to suspect his domestic rivals or opponents of making common cause against him with the leaders of the foreign communist parties, particularly those of the powerful German party. For these same reasons, he was generally hesitant to encourage foreign communist parties to attempt to seize power. He was, moreover, an extremely cautious and wary man, disinclined to commit himself to any open contest unless the odds were strongly on his side. He tended to place even greater stress than Lenin on the preservation of "the base"—that is, the integrity of Soviet power in Russia, where he felt relatively secure.

The enmity he bore toward the western "bourgeois" world was no less fierce and uncompromising than that of Lenin and his other associates in the movement; but it stemmed more from a general cultural unfamiliarity with the West, and fear of its physical and intellectual strength, than from ideological convictions. His hopes for the advancement of Soviet power rested primarily on two factors over which he felt himself in a position to exert greater personal control than over revolutionary activities of foreign communist parties. The first of these was the expansion of Russia's own industrial and military power. The second was the exploitation of the differences between the great powers of the capitalist world. His temperament inclined him, in all the encounters of life—personal as well as political—to seek the promotion of his purposes not by direct confrontation with his opponents but by pitting them against each other and causing them to waste their strength in mutual struggle, to a point where he could profit from their exhaustion and could intervene, without great risk, to impose his terms in the end. This, the exploitation of divisive factors in the enemy camp, was the essence of his statesmanship. His diplomacy became, with time, a single undeviating effort to embroil other great powers against each other to the advantage of the movement he controlled and personified. What he asked of the foreign communist parties was not that they should seize power, but that they should become the willing, self-effacing, and self-sacrificing agents of a Soviet diplomacy directed primarily to the preservation of his own personal position, and to the expansion of the territory under his personal control.[1]

In the immediate aftermath of Lenin's death, Stalin and his leading colleagues were extensively occupied with the problem of succession. For some time Chicherin was permitted to function with relative independence at the Foreign Affairs Commissariat. During this period the Commissariat, insofar as it had independent power to affect Soviet policy, carried on in the traditions and concepts of the Lenin era. But Chicherin, close as he was to the Right opposition, had no intimacy with Stalin, whose power was at that time being quietly built up in

[1] A good idea of the concepts with which Stalin approached the tasks of formulating Soviet foreign policy may be had from the lecture which he delivered at the Sverdlovsk University, shortly after Lenin's death, on the subject of "The Strategy and Tactics of the Revolution." Excerpts will be found in *Document No. 16.*

the inner recesses of the Party and the secret police. It was not long before this lack of intimacy began to lead to uncoordinated actions in matters affecting foreign affairs. The Commissariat for Foreign Affairs suffered particularly, then and at all times during the Stalin era, from an inability to exert authority or influence over the treatment of foreign representatives and nationals within Russia—a province jealously kept and guarded by the secret police. The years following Lenin's death were studded with instances in which relations with one country or another would be damaged by independent actions of the Soviet secret police, designed to bolster either its own political ambitions or those of Stalin and the Party leadership, but in conflict with the general pattern of Soviet foreign policy. Precisely because internal security was at all times placed ahead of foreign affairs in importance, the secret police achieved a position, especially in matters affecting foreigners within Russia, which would constitute throughout the Stalin era a frequent and serious impediment to the development of good relations with other states.

***De Jure* Recognition.** Lenin's death coincided closely in time with the general collapse of the resistance of the noncommunist world to full *de jure* recognition of the Soviet government. Here the lead was given by Britain.[2]

Throughout the immediate postwar years, the Labour party in Britain had favored rapid development of relations with Moscow. In particular, a well-organized left-wing group within the party, entitled the "Hands Off Russia Committee," had been active in putting out propaganda in support of Soviet positions and in opposing the British government in the intervention policy as well as in subsequent issues of disagreement with Moscow.

The violent debates over the Curzon ultimatum, in the spring and summer of 1923, forced the Labour party into an even more extreme pro-Soviet position than it would perhaps otherwise have taken. In the autumn of 1923 there occurred the change of government which brought

[2] It is probable that certain governments, outstandingly Italy, would have recognized Russia in the immediately ensuing period, even had Britain not done so. But the British example was of outstanding importance.

the Labour party to power under the premiership of Ramsay MacDonald. In the preceding election campaign the Labour party had committed itself unreservedly to full and unconditional recognition of the Soviet government. On assuming office, it had no choice, therefore, but to take this step, which it did on February 2, 1924.

The example was followed a few days later (February 8) by Italy. (Mussolini had already, some weeks earlier, indicated his intention to make the move.) A number of other governments, including those of France and Japan, followed suit within the year. The United States still remained aloof, as did some of the smaller countries, notably Yugoslavia and Switzerland. But the Labour government's action signified the official acceptance of the Soviet government, at least on the formal diplomatic level, by a large and important segment of the capitalist world.

The beginning of the post-Lenin era thus coincided with the achievement of one of the main objectives to which Soviet diplomacy had theretofore been addressed.

**First Consequences of British Recognition.** Recognition of the Soviet government by Great Britain did not, as it turned out, produce that era of good feeling and rapid development in the relations between the two governments which its advocates had anticipated. As a result, presumably, of its own parliamentary weakness (it commanded a majority only in coalition with the Liberals) and of the need for the collaboration of business and financial circles in any revival of Anglo-Russian economic relations, the Labour government saw itself obliged, immediately after recognizing the Soviet government, to enter into negotiations with Soviet representatives for a General Treaty which should involve a settlement of the tangled and confusing question of debts and claims. In the conduct of these negotiations, it had to give heed to the views and requirements of legal and financial experts of the British government, as well as to those of leading private bankers. The result was that the negotiations soon bogged down in the complexities of the practically insoluble problem of debts and claims. The Soviet government, having now achieved full diplomatic recognition both from the German and the British governments without making substantial prior concessions in these matters, naturally saw no reason to make such concessions once recognition had been achieved. The result was that, in early August 1924, the Anglo-Soviet negotiations, which had begun in April, reached a point of complete breakdown. The outstanding difficulty was, as usual, the question of compensation for British property in Russia nationalized in the course of the revolution. Through the last-minute intercession of a number of Labour members of Parliament, the break was patched up, but only by the device of agreeing to defer the disputed question for further negotiation at some time in the future. The treaty, devoid of provisions for the settlement of these matters, was then signed, and laid before Parliament for ratification.

**The Zinoviev Letter.** Before the treaty could be ratified, the government was successfully challenged in Parliament, not over the issue of the treaty itself but over its alleged lenience in prosecuting a charge of seditious libel against the editor of one of the organs of the British Communist Party. New elections were at once scheduled. But in the interval before they could take place an episode occurred which substantially affected their outcome.

On October 24, 1924, in the midst of the election campaign, the Chief of the Northern Department of the Foreign Office, Mr. J. D. Gregory, addressed to the Soviet Chargé d'Affaires a strong note of protest over a letter alleged to have been written by the well-known Soviet figure, G. E. Zinoviev, in his capacity as titular head of the Comintern, to the Central Committee of the British Communist Party. Copies of the note and of the alleged letter were released to the press by the Foreign Office, that same day. The text of the letter had already reached the Conservative press in London from independent sources.

The letter, as allegedly written by Zinoviev, was sharply hostile to the leaders of the Labour party. It called for instigation of revolutionary action in Ireland and in the colonies. It instructed the British communists to establish secret cells within the British armed forces. Its tenor, in short, was embarrassing in the extreme to the Labour government. It could not fail to pour oil on the fire of the Conservative attack on the government, and to discredit even in the minds of Labour's supporters the policy of accommodation with the Soviet Union.

The original of this document has never been produced. Not even the British government claims to have seen it. A number of the detailed points, and in some respects the wording, suggest strongly that it was a forgery. The Prime Minister, Mr. Ramsay MacDonald, was not in London when the note was despatched, and his own degree of responsibility for this step and for the implied acceptance of the authenticity of the document have never been fully clarified. The subsequent handling of the matter on the part of the British government was not such as to suggest any strong conviction on its part that the document was authentic.

There was, however, little time for the public to become aware of these odd circumstances in the period between publication of the letter and the election, which took place on October 29. As the result of the election, the strength of the Labour party in Parliament was reduced from 191 to 151, and the Conservatives were brought back into power. That the outcome of the election was to some extent affected by the "Zinoviev letter" seems not generally to be disputed, though recent researches suggest that the effect was smaller than originally supposed. On November 21, 1924, the new Baldwin government announced its unwillingness to sponsor the still unratified Anglo-Soviet General Treaty. In this way, the entire effort at a post-recognition accommodation, introduced by the MacDonald government, came to naught.

**The Problem of European Security.** Meanwhile, there had begun in western Europe that process of accommodation between Germany and the western powers which liquidated the unhappy episode of the Ruhr occupation and brought Germany into an acceptable economic and psychological relationship with the French and British, as well as to membership in the League of Nations. The Dawes Plan, designed to achieve at least a provisional settlement of the reparations problem and to lay a foundation for economic reconstruction in Europe, was worked out in the winter and spring of 1924. It entered into effect on September 1. With it went efforts, particularly on the British side, to patch up the political relationships among the European powers in a manner that would permit Germany's entry into the League of Nations and would afford security to both Germany and her neighbors to the West. This undertaking was pursued with particular seriousness by the new Conservative government in England, immediately following its assumption of office at the turn of the year 1924-1925.

The German government, under Stresemann's leadership, was quite prepared to explore these possibilities, provided always that it could retain its freedom to pursue a policy of peaceful revisionism with respect to Germany's frontiers in the East. It therefore took advantage of British hints in this direction, and embarked, in February 1925, on the series of diplomatic exchanges and talks which led to the conclusion, in the autumn of that year, of the so-called Locarno treaties.[3] These instruments guaranteed Germany's western frontiers and provided for mutual assistance obligations between France, on the one hand, and Poland and Czechoslovakia, on the other.

An integral part of the Locarno settlement was the agreement that Germany should apply for entry into the League of Nations. This the German government did in March 1925. Due to difficulties which arose over the question of Germany's having one of the permanent seats on the League Council, German membership did not, however, become a reality until the summer of 1926.

**Soviet Opposition to Western Security Arrangements.** The Soviet government took an attitude of extreme suspicion and displeasure toward this entire process of regularization of Germany's relationship to the other western powers. On the overt level, its propagandists kept up a steady drumfire of efforts to discredit the new arrangements that were under discussion, to sow dissension and distrust among the various western powers, and to convince the Germans, in particular, that accommodation to the West, along the contemplated lines, would lead to Germany's undoing. In private talks and negotiations with the German government, Soviet officials used every conceivable sort of blandishment and threat to deflect Strese-

[3] The Locarno documents were initialed on October 15, 1925, and signed in London on December 1 of that year.

mann from his purpose. They offered, as an alternative, a full-fledged alliance, directed against Poland. They suggested the conclusion of a secret agreement not to enter into any political or economic alliances or understandings with third powers, to be supplemented by an understanding that the two parties would follow a common policy with respect to the League of Nations. When these proposals proved unacceptable to the German government, they pressed the less drastic device of a neutrality pact. Throughout these secret conversations, proceeding during the year 1925 and the beginning of 1926, they never ceased to hint that if Germany refused these Soviet offers and continued on her path of rapprochement with the West, Russia might counter by arriving at an agreement with the French and the Poles which would guarantee the existing German-Polish border, in return for concessions with respect to Poland's border with Russia.

In general, the Germans did not permit themselves to be deflected from their path by this Russian pressure. But certain concessions were made to soften Soviet discontent.

In 1924 and 1925, a major commercial treaty had been under negotiation between the Russians and the Germans. As of the summer of 1925 the negotiations were not yet completed. To weaken the sting of the Locarno treaties, the Germans went ahead and signed this commercial treaty on October 12, 1925. The announcement of its forthcoming signature was made by Stresemann on the day of his departure for Locarno. This served as a reminder to the world public that the conclusion of the Locarno agreements did not mean the abandonment of the Rapallo policy.

Secondly, the Germans, as a response to the Soviet pressures and in deference to the strong feelings of Brockdorff-Rantzau, coupled their entry into the League with conditions designed to offset Soviet fears. Even more than by the Locarno pacts themselves, the Russians were frightened (or professed to be) by the possible operation of Article 16 of the League Covenant, which obliged member-states to render any possible aid to any other state that might become a victim of aggression, and to permit passage through their territory of the armed forces of any other member acting in pursuit of a decision of the League. The Russians saw, in Germany's acceptance of this obligation, an undertaking on Germany's part to collaborate (by permitting French passage through German territory) in a future Franco-Polish attack on Russia. The German government met this anxiety on the Soviet side by insisting, vis-à-vis the western powers, on a proviso to their entry into the League of Nations to the effect that any contribution Germany might make under Article 16 would be limited to "the degree which geographical position and particular situation as regard armaments allow." It was generally understood that this vague reservation would leave Germany free to refuse to permit passage of French troops across her territory to the East.

Finally, when in March 1926 the French and the Poles held up German entry into the League by their opposition to allowing Germany a permanent seat on the Council, the German government, to which this development brought keen disillusionment and embarrassment, corrected the balance by going ahead and signing on April 24, 1926, the so-called "Berlin Treaty" for which the Russians had been pressing. This was a neutrality pact, specifically reaffirming the Rapallo relationship, providing for neutrality if either party should be attacked by a third party, and banning participation in any international action along the lines of an economic or financial boycott of the other party.

The Soviet government did not profess itself satisfied with these concessions, but they served to offset in some degree the political effects of the German rapprochement with the West. The rapprochement, in any case, produced in the end no dramatically unfavorable effect on Soviet-German relations. Both Russians and Germans had by this time learned to take a more sober estimate of the possibilities of their mutual relationship. The Germans, for their part, had never fully recovered from the shock of the communist action in Germany of October 1923. They noted with misgivings the growing signs of isolation of the relatively pro-German Chicherin from the inner Party circles. The Russians, on the other hand, learned from the tenor of German policy from 1923 to 1926 that the German government was not willing to sacrifice to the demands of the Rapallo spirit any favorable possibilities for the improvement of German relations with the western powers and for overcoming the isolation of Versailles. They were forced to recognize that they could not, by means of the Rapallo agreement, bind the Germans to a position that would preclude in any and all circumstances a united front of the Germans and the western powers in matters of interest to them.

**The Break with England.** The period following the return of the English Conservatives to power at the end of 1924 was marked by a continued deterioration of Anglo-Soviet relations. The strong anti-Soviet feeling already existing in conservative circles in England found further sustenance in the sympathy and support extended by Moscow to the British coal miners in the labor difficulties of 1926, and in the similar support given at that time (see Chapter 6) to the Kuomintang in China. On top of these difficulties there appears also to have been a certain change of heart on the part of some of the major private claimants against the Soviet government, particularly Mr. Leslie Urquhart, head of the Russian-Asiatic Consolidated Company, Limited (see p. 51). These claimants, having failed to get satisfaction of their claims by negotiation with the Soviet government, now swung over to a position in favor of a complete rupture of Anglo-Soviet relations.

From the beginning of 1926, there were evidences that the British government was moving toward a break. The matter achieved a certain urgency due to the fact that private British bankers were beginning at that time to give serious consideration to the extension of private banking credit to the Soviet Foreign Trade Monopoly. Only a strong line of official policy could avert this development.

On May 12, 1927, the British authorities raided the premises both of the Soviet Trade Delegation (which, in accordance with the trade agreement of 1921, was supposed to enjoy extraterritoriality), and those of the official Soviet trading company, Arcos. The raid apparently failed to yield any very incriminating evidence. The British government nevertheless proceeded on May 26, 1927, to sever all official relations with Russia.

Relations were not resumed until after the return of the Labour party to power in the general elections of May 30, 1929. Negotiations between the two governments were taken up that summer. On October 1, 1929, agreement on the resumption of relations was announced. By the end of that year the new exchange of ambassadors had been effected.

**Effect of European Reverses on Soviet Policy Generally.** The reverses suffered by the Soviet government, first in the failure of the revolutionary action in Germany in late 1923, second in the Locarno settlements, and third in the deterioration of relations with England under the Conservative government, all tended to produce in Moscow a general disillusionment with the prospects for Soviet diplomacy in the West. The natural corollary of this disillusionment was a heightened interest in the possibilities which, by the year 1923, had begun to become visible on Russia's eastern horizon.

— 6 —

# ASIA, TO 1935

**General Motivations of Soviet Policy in Asia.** The situation that confronted the Soviet leaders in East Asia, as they assumed responsibility for the conduct of the external affairs of the Russian state, was one of such extreme confusion and complexity that neither from the ideological nor from the practical standpoint did any clear guide-lines of policy present themselves.

With the exception of Japan, the countries of the Far East were industrialized only to a negligible degree. The prerequisites for socialist revolution in the Marxist sense were not present. There were only the tiniest rudiments of an industrial proletariat. There was not even an indigenous capitalism, in the Marxian sense. Here, there could be no question of any immediate social revolution.

Most of these countries, on the other hand, were either colonial dependencies of European powers or were regarded in Moscow as being in a state of economic vassalage and dependence to western (and, in the case of China, Japanese as well) imperialists. The beginnings of the national-liberation movement, stimulated by the stresses of the World War, were already visible at the time of the Bolshevik seizure of power in Petrograd. It was Lenin's view (and this became generally authoritative for the Soviet regime) that the Russian communists, while encouraging and awaiting the development in Asia of the prerequisites for true social revolution, should lend all possible support to the national-liberation movements, even if this meant temporary collaboration with classes other than the industrial proletariat, particularly the peasantry, the petty bourgeoisie, and the liberal intellectuals. If the Asian peoples could be brought in this way to sever the bonds of their dependence on the capitalist world and to drive the foreign "imperialists" from their midst, this would not, to be sure, alone produce the European revolution on which Russian communist hopes were set, but it would add greatly to the internal stresses and contradictions of western capitalism and would thus help materially to tip the scales in favor of social revolution in the West. (*See Document No. 17.*)

In addition to this basic ideological motivation, the Soviet leaders had also to concern themselves from the start for their own military and political security—for protection of that "base" of world socialism which Russia, under their rule, appeared to them to represent. This, too, demanded the maximum elimination from Asia, and particularly from regions adjacent to the borders of the Soviet state, of the influence of the great western powers and of Japan. In this sense, it coincided with the demands of the national-liberation movement. But it also coincided very largely with the motives which had animated the Tsarist regime in its policies toward Asia. Particularly along the Chinese border, since there was at this time no Chinese central government strong enough to be presumed capable of assuming effective power in any areas from which "imperialist" control might be eliminated—in other words, since the only conceivable substitute for the predominance of one great external power in these bordering regions was the predominance of another—the Soviet government found itself obliged to seek, and to assume within the limits of practical possibility, much the same special positions of privilege and power as the Tsarist government had enjoyed, thus substituting in effect its own "imperialism" for that which had been eliminated.

**The Middle East.** With relation to the three Moslem states along Russia's southern border—Turkey, Iran, and Afghanistan—Soviet policy in the period between the two world wars was directed and restricted largely to the promotion of nationalistic and anti-imperialistic tendencies, as a check to the influence of Britain. Of the three countries, it was Turkey, with its highly strategic situation, which provided the most active and important problem for Soviet policy.

The Turkish nationalist movement under Kemal Pasha, which fought its way to power in the immediate post-hostilities period by way of reaction and opposition to the severely punitive peace (reminiscent of Brest-Litovsk) which the Allies attempted to impose upon Turkey, commanded strong sympathy in Moscow, particularly in Lenin's time. The Soviet government concluded a treaty of friendship with the new Turkish regime in 1921 (March 16), gave it considerable military aid in its struggle with the Greeks and the western Allies, and was, as we have seen, more Turkish than the Turks in the position it adopted at the Lausanne Conference. In later years the relationship between the two countries, to be sure, generally fell short of an entire cordiality. It was troubled by Comintern activities in Turkey, by a latent conflict of aspiration with regard to certain border regions, and by the relative coldness and suspicion with which Stalin, himself a Georgian, viewed these neighbors of the Soviet Trans-Caucasus. But in general Soviet-Turkish relations remained down to World War II a reverse function of the differences both parties had with the western powers; and these differences were, by and large, sufficient to assure an outwardly even, and at times even markedly favorable, course of the Turkish-Soviet relationship.

Thus in 1925, as a reaction on the Soviet side to the Locarno Treaties, and on the Turkish side to the unfavorable Mosul settlement, the two countries demonstratively signed (December 16) a neutrality pact which came close to being an outright alliance. The first Soviet effort in the way of technical and economic aid to an underdeveloped area consisted of help to the Turks, in the mid-thirties, in the building of a textile industry. And when, in 1936, the Turks called for a new revision of the regime of the Straits, the Soviet government supported strongly, at the ensuing Montreux Conference, the right of the Turks to fortify and control the waterway. Only after the change of Soviet policy in Europe, in 1939, did the Soviet government espouse the imperialistic ambitions for Russian military control of the Straits by which Tsarist policy had once been inspired—a change which brought it for the first time into sharp political conflict with Turkish national interests.

The relationship with Iran and Afghanistan took its general tone from the relationship with Turkey. With these countries, too, treaties of friendship were signed early in 1921. Here, too, there were initial border rivalries and differences to be overcome,[1] and subsequent relations were occasionally troubled by Comintern intrigues. But the governments of the two smaller countries had a stake in the cultivation of the relationship with Moscow as a counterbalance to the influence of England; and Moscow, for its part, was generally content to place the emphasis of its diplomatic and political effort in this region on anti-imperialist and national-liberationist goals.

**The Liquidation of Japanese Intervention.** In East Asia, the most immediate and urgent problem of Soviet policy in the period following the revolution was the liquidation of Japanese intervention in the Russian Far East. When the American forces withdrew from Siberia, in the winter and spring of 1920, the Japanese attempted to tighten their hold on the Maritime Province, and proceeded in addition to seize Northern Sakhalin. Now, for the first time, they were able to pursue, without major

[1] In 1920, an unsuccessful attempt was made by Stalin, in his capacity as Commissar for Nationalities, to bring a portion of Northern Iran under direct Soviet control.

interference by the United States, the aims which had initially inspired their intervention in that area. But the collapse of Kolchak's regime, and the political failure of the Russian Cossack leaders whom the Japanese had employed as the principal puppets of their power in eastern Siberia, left them devoid of a political basis for their presence in Siberia. Intervention could continue, now, only in the form of an indefinite military occupation of a hostile territory. The presence of the Japanese forces in Siberia served, moreover, as a serious impediment to the regularization of Japan's relations with the western powers and with China. In 1922, consequently, the Japanese finally found themselves obliged to withdraw from the Siberian mainland. They continued, for the time being, to hold on to Northern Sakhalin, primarily as a bargaining asset for the pending regularization of their relations with the Soviet government. The Japanese forces were withdrawn from Northern Sakhalin only in 1925, as part of a general settlement which, in addition to providing for the establishment of full diplomatic relations between Japan and the Soviet regime, gave the Japanese oil concessions in that region, as well as important privileges with relation to fishing along the Siberian coast.

The Soviet part in bringing about the end of Japanese intervention had consisted principally in the vigorous and successful prosecution of the civil war in Siberia, and the bombardment of the Japanese government with a constant stream of diplomatic protests and pressures, accompanied by patient and persistent negotiation.

**The Securing of Outer Mongolia.** In this same period the Soviet government found it necessary to take energetic action to protect its interests in Outer Mongolia. In the final years of Tsarist power, this area had been a Russian protectorate. In the period from 1917 to 1920, it was the scene of considerable activity on the part of Russian anti-Bolshevik elements, under the leadership of the Ataman Semenov and (later) Baron Ungern-Sternberg, who were reputed to enjoy (and generally did) Japanese support. The Soviet government, just completing its hard-earned victory in the civil war at home, could not afford to leave this highly strategic area, so close to the strategically sensitive "Baikal barrier" of the Trans-Siberian

Railway, in the hands of violently anti-Bolshevik Russian figures. The fact that the Trans-Baikal region of Siberia contained a considerable population of Mongolian origin added to the danger.

Early in 1921, Ungern-Sternberg seized the Outer Mongolian center of Urga. Efforts to enlist the collaboration of the Chinese government in suppressing him having failed, the Russians took characteristic action. They stimulated the establishment in Outer Mongolia of a pro-communist faction which, in the summer of 1921, appealed formally to the Soviet government for assistance. This request was immediately granted; a Soviet military force was despatched; Ungern-Sternberg was captured and shot; a puppet government, noncommunist but wholly under Soviet domination (the forerunner of the "People's Democracies" of a later day), was established. A political treaty was concluded between the Soviet government and this new Mongolian regime on November 5, 1921. At the formal request of the latter, Soviet forces remained in Outer Mongolia until 1924.

For reasons of political prudence, the fact of Chinese sovereignty in Outer Mongolia was, at that time, not yet questioned. But Moscow insisted that the area was fully autonomous, and that the new Mongolian regime had the right to manifest its independence vis-à-vis Peking in matters of foreign policy and defense.

**The Peking Government.** At the time of the Russian revolution, China was in a state of great political confusion. Central government had broken down completely. It would scarcely be an exaggeration to say that there were nearly as many centers of political power in China at that time as there were warlords. But two of these centers stood out: Peking, in the north, still the seat of the regime that was nominally the government of China and was recognized as such by the Powers; and Canton, in the south, where Sun Yat-sen, the father of the earlier Chinese revolution of 1911, had established himself under local warlord protection, with a band of ideological followers associated in the political organization known as the Kuomintang.

The Soviet leaders were anxious to establish regular diplomatic relations with the Peking regime for the same reasons that caused them to seek such relations with the governments of the great western powers—because, that is, they hoped that it would enable them to stabilize and protect their position in East Asia. Besides, the Peking government represented in their eyes an agency through which one could exert influence on China with a view to causing her to assert her independence in the face of the imperialist powers.

Moscow was never averse to framing its policies in such a way as to appeal to peoples, over the heads of governments, with a view to bringing pressure on the respective governments to comply with Soviet desiderata. Thus the first acts of the Soviet government with relation to China consisted in the issuance of proclamations professing its fraternal friendship and solicitude for the Chinese people, denouncing unequal treaties by which China had previously been bound to Russia, renouncing all the privileges and rights those treaties had provided, as well as all annexations of Chinese territory. With regard to the Chinese-Eastern Railway,[2] the Soviet government offered to conclude a special treaty governing the future mode of operation of this enterprise.

In 1921 and 1922, missions were despatched to Peking to press for a treaty establishing diplomatic relations on this basis. But the Peking regime, itself extensively dependent on foreign support, was, like the German government until 1922, reluctant to move faster than the western governments in regularizing relations with Soviet Russia. For the time, it resisted the Soviet initiative, holding out for the prior withdrawal of Soviet forces from Outer Mongolia and for a complete transfer of the Chinese-Eastern Railway to China.

This recalcitrance on the part of Peking was no doubt

[2] This railway, running through Chinese territory in Manchuria, had, before the revolution, been under effective Russian control and operation. It was virtually owned by the Russian Treasury. Initially, in 1919, while still in the throes of the civil war, the Soviet government rashly offered to turn over the line, together with all the contingent rights and concessions Russia had enjoyed in the railway zone, to "the Chinese people." (*See Document No. 18.*) But this offer was soon disavowed by Soviet negotiators, and replaced by the more prudent one described above.

one of the factors which impelled Moscow, at the end of 1922, to shift the emphasis of its policy to south China and to undertake a major effort to build up the Kuomintang as the principal political force and vehicle for Soviet policy in the country. To this end, a special representative of the Soviet government, Michael Borodin, was despatched to South China in 1923 to act as adviser to the Kuomintang.

This switch of interest to South China served as an effective warning that Moscow would not be lacking in alternatives if Peking continued to be unreceptive to Soviet advances. The withdrawal of Japanese troops from the Soviet mainland in 1922 also strengthened Moscow's hand. When, therefore, the Soviet government despatched to Peking, in the summer of 1923, a senior negotiator in the person of L. M. Karakhan, an Assistant Commissar for Foreign Affairs, negotiations began in earnest. Formal difficulties were removed, from the Chinese standpoint, by the establishment of diplomatic relations between Britain and the U.S.S.R. in February 1924. By dint of these circumstances, and of his own very considerable diplomatic skill, Karakhan finally achieved the conclusion, on May 31, 1924, of a treaty providing for the establishment of diplomatic relations on terms generally favorable to Soviet interests. To be sure, the Soviet government undertook to withdraw its forces from Outer Mongolia;[3] but it had now had time to train Mongolian forces to take their place, and the new Mongolian force remained under direct Soviet control. As for the Chinese-Eastern, the settlement included arrangements for a joint provisional management of the railway, in which the Chinese were to have nominal, the Russians real, control.

**Stalin's Failure with the Kuomintang.** However, the switch of emphasis in 1922 and 1923 from the north to the south of China had represented something more in Soviet policy than just a tactical maneuver. Moscow was seriously interested in building up the Kuomintang as an effective anti-imperialist force. This effort was carried forward with great vigor and with considerable success during the years 1923-1926. Under Borodin's guidance, the Kuo-

[3] The withdrawal was completed by March 1925.

mintang was developed during these years from an ineffective group of intellectuals into a well-organized military-political movement. It was patterned organizationally after the Russian Communist Party, but took its ideological inspiration from the teachings of Sun Yat-sen, and was thus not based (as would have been a true communist party) exclusively on the "toilers." Great pains were taken to assure that the organization was provided with an independent military arm which could become an effective instrument of civil conflict. One of the more promising of the younger officers associated with the Kuomintang, Chiang Kai-shek, was brought to Moscow in 1923 for several months of training in Soviet methods. Upon his return to China, he founded and directed at Canton the Whampoa Military Academy, where the training of an officers corps for the Kuomintang forces was undertaken.

There can be no question but that, in pursuing this strengthening and development of the Kuomintang, Stalin had in mind Lenin's view that China was not yet in any way prepared for social revolution in the Marxist sense. He was concerned primarily to create in China a strong nationalist force which would take an effective stand against the "imperialist" powers, and could thus constitute an ally of Soviet Russia against the British and the Japanese. The rejection by Parliament of the Anglo-Soviet treaty in late 1924, the return of the Conservatives to power at that time (see p. 59), and the subsequent deterioration of Anglo-Soviet relations, all served to inflame Stalin's easily inflammable suspicions; and there seems little doubt that he overrated, throughout those years, the danger of a revival under British auspices of the intervention of 1918-1920. (*See Documents Nos. 19 and 20.*) He was particularly concerned, therefore, to weaken England and to engage her attentions in another area.

It was recognized, of course, that there were elements among the Chinese bourgeoisie who had a stake in the preservation of the influence and the economic positions of the capitalist powers in China, and who had therefore to be opposed rather than supported. The Peking regime, despite the advantages to be gained by its recognition, was considered to be largely and increasingly representative of such elements, and thus unpromising as a primary vehicle for Soviet policy. But there was another portion of the bourgeoisie (generally, the poorer portion) which was considered sincerely anti-imperialistic and available for development, together with workers and peasants, as the basis for a national movement. All these elements, it was hoped, could be united under the banner of the Kuomintang.

Such an effort posed delicate problems with respect to the Chinese Communist Party. At the time of its foundation in 1921, this party had represented only a handful of intellectuals. But by 1924, under the tutelage of Comintern agents, it had gained strength and had even come to command certain positions of more than negligible political importance in the labor union movement. Moscow could not, as a matter of principle, refrain from encouraging its growth. Yet this party could not be permitted to take a strictly revolutionary stance that would place it in sharp opposition to the bourgeois or other nonproletarian elements within the Kuomintang. Means had to be found to fit the Chinese communist movement into the Kuomintang in such a way that it would neither lose its own identity and its revolutionary potential for the more distant future nor embarrass and antagonize the nonproletarian majority within the Kuomintang ranks. (*See Document No. 21.*)

For over three years Borodin, under anxious tutelage from the Kremlin, struggled with this delicate and difficult problem. The resulting questions of policy often constituted a subject of anguished and heated controversy among the Soviet leaders themselves, particularly between Stalin and Trotsky. There can be no doubt, as seen now from the vantage point of over three decades, that Stalin went too far in forcing the Chinese communists to lose themselves in the Kuomintang organization and to subordinate themselves to the power of the noncommunist political and military leaders within that movement.

By the beginning of 1926, there were already ominous signs of a growing divergence of interest and ambition as between the bourgeois elements in the Kuomintang and the Chinese communists. In the spring of that year, Chiang seized effective leadership of the movement, in Canton, and took measures to bring the communist element within the organization under closer control. Despite these evidences of growing disunity, the decision was taken shortly thereafter to launch a military expedition to the north with a view to widening the area under the Kuomintang control. The expedition began in June 1926. It proceeded with conspicuous success up to the spring of 1927, bringing most of China south of the Yangtze, as well as the great Yangtze ports, under Kuomintang control. But the stress of these developments put an even greater strain on the unity within the movement. As Chiang consolidated his power along the Yangtze, he undertook various repressive measures against the communists, culminating finally in a series of bloody reprisals which decimated the party's ranks and virtually drove it underground. In July 1927, the party was formally expelled from the Kuomintang. Borodin was compelled to abandon his mission and return to Russia.

Having rid himself in this way of his communist allies, Chiang proceeded to consolidate his rule throughout China and to set up a new all-Chinese government, recognized by the Powers, at Nanking. It was not until December 1932 that the Soviet government was able to establish full diplomatic relations with this new regime.

This series of events constituted something little short of a major disaster from Moscow's standpoint. Soviet efforts had indeed succeeded in stimulating the creation of a new national government in China, and one which was to a certain extent anti-imperialistic; but it had wholly lost control over this movement, and in its misguided effort to control it, it had largely sacrificed the Chinese communist movement of the day. True, Mao Tse-tung and his associates were able, without Russian help, to rescue a portion of the communist organization, to build it up again, and eventually to move it laboriously around the western periphery of China to the north where it would find new possibilities for development in the period of World War II. But much damage had been done, meanwhile, to Russian prestige. The Trotskyites, who had been so critical of Stalin's policies in China, had had their moment of triumph. A distrust of

Moscow's leadership had been generated in the minds of the Chinese communist leadership which must be assumed to have endured to the present day.

**Conflict over the Chinese-Eastern Railway.** It was perhaps only natural that following this successful rebuff to Moscow's efforts to play a role in Chinese internal affairs, renewed efforts should have been made to wrest the Chinese-Eastern Railway from Russian control. In late 1928 the Chinese authorities in Manchuria began to make trouble for the Russian administration of the railway. In July 1929 they attempted to seize the enterprise entirely. In doing so they neglected to recall that Russia's military situation was quite different with relation to the Manchurian area than it was in relation to South China. In November 1929, the Russians, seizing two points on the Chinese-Russian border, staged a military demonstration which convinced the Chinese of the seriousness of their determination not to permit themselves to be displaced from their control of the railway. This sufficed to bring the Chinese to heel. The following month an agreement was reached between the two parties, which left the railway in Russian hands.

The tensions produced by this incident, involving even the complete severance of diplomatic relations between Moscow and Peking, served to delay the establishment of anything resembling a normal relationship between Russia and China.

It was in connection with this Chinese attempt to seize the Chinese-Eastern Railway that Secretary of State Stimson endeavored to bring pressure on the contestants to keep the peace by invoking the provisions of the Pact of Paris (generally referred to as the Kellogg Pact) for the Outlawry of War. This ill-advised step (taken actually on the very day that the Chinese and the Russians composed their basic differences) gave the Soviet government an opportunity to make a stinging reply to Washington, rejecting the interference and emphasizing the abnormality of the continued absence of diplomatic relations between the United States and Russia. (*See Document No. 22.*)

**The Japanese Seizure of Manchuria.** Although Russia was successful in retaining the Chinese-Eastern Railway in 1929, her very success in doing so was, insofar as it exposed the extreme weakness of the Chinese, probably instrumental in evoking a new and greater threat from another quarter. In 1931 Japan undertook what was virtually the conquest of the entire Manchurian area. By the end of 1932, this operation was successfully completed. The Chinese-Eastern Railway, still under Russian management, could now operate only by Japanese tolerance.

The Soviet government, too weak to challenge the Japanese action, showed great restraint, and did all in its power to avoid becoming involved in conflict with Japan. It did, however, react in several ways. It resumed relations with the Chinese government (December 1932). It intensified its efforts to win American recognition, with a view to bringing America's influence into the scales as a factor of restraint on Japanese policy. It pursued a vigorous development of its own armed forces in eastern Siberia. It issued a series of sharp warnings to Japan that any violation of Soviet frontiers would mean full-fledged war.

**The Sale of the Chinese-Eastern Railway.** These measures sufficed to avert any Japanese movement into Siberia itself. They were not sufficient, however, to preserve Russia's rights on the Chinese-Eastern Railway. Early in 1933, the Japanese, exploiting their new position of ascendancy in Manchuria, began to make serious trouble for the Soviet management of the railway. There was now nothing Moscow could do. To resist the Japanese encroachments meant to risk involvement in a war for which Russia was not prepared. To tolerate it meant to lose prestige and to permit Russia's assets in Manchuria to be exploited by the Japanese to Russia's own disadvantage. With great reluctance the decision was taken to sell the Russian stake in the railway to the Japanese puppet regime in Manchuria—and thus in effect to the Japanese. Negotiations to this end, undertaken in June 1933, dragged on until March 1935, when the sale was finally completed. The Soviet government received, in the end, only a pittance for its stake in the road. But it succeeded, through the long process of negotiation, in softening the blow to its own prestige.

In this way the Japanese, taking advantage of the weakness of both Russia and China, succeeded in 1935 in wiping out all the gains made by Russian policy in Manchuria since the construction of the Trans-Siberian Railway at the end of the nineteenth century. The Soviet government, in the face of a disorganized economy and military unpreparedness, could do no more than to guard its own frontiers and to strive desperately, by every means at its disposal, to stimulate the Chinese, the British, and the Americans to resist Japan's expansionist policies and thus to lead Japanese energies into another direction. This policy Moscow pursued consistently and, despite many crises and dangers, successfully, down to the very day of the Japanese attack on Pearl Harbor.

Throughout the 1930's, the Japanese menace remained probably the dominant foreign-political reality on the Moscow horizon. The reactions of Stalin and his associates to events in Europe during this period will not be intelligible unless this sense of extreme danger on the eastern frontier of their power is borne in mind.

— 7 —

# THE RISE OF EUROPEAN FASCISM

**The Five Year Plan.** The year 1927, as we have seen, brought failure and frustration to Soviet policies both in Europe, where the rupture of relations with Britain was a major blow, and in Asia, where catastrophe befell the Chinese communists as a consequence of Soviet policy. These events combined with internal developments within Russia to produce a certain reorientation of Soviet policy. In the ensuing period the Soviet government turned its back even more resolutely than before on actual revolutionary activities abroad, retired into a semi-isolation, and devoted its efforts to the accomplishment of two great internal programs.

One of these was the launching of a major effort of industrial construction, designed to turn Russia into a modern industrial and military power. Such an undertaking had long been the demand of the Left opposition. Now, with Trotsky finally expelled from the Party, Stalin could launch such a program under his own auspices, without seeming to be yielding to opposition pressures. To the outside world, the initial phase of this effort, despite the real emphasis on military industry, was presented as a program for the general peaceful development of the Russian economy, and was given the name of the First Five Year Plan.

The second of the two great undertakings of that period was the effort to establish a tight control over agricultural production, in order to assure at all times the feeding of the cities and the army. This was to be accomplished by forcing the mass of the Russian peasantry into collective farms, a measure which, it was hoped, would also have the advantage of facilitating the introduction of agricultural machinery into the Russian countryside.

These two measures—the Five Year Plan and collectivization—dominated Soviet policy throughout the years from 1928 to 1933.[1] Pressed forward crudely and recklessly, with abundant use of force and with an appalling wastage of human and physical resources, they sufficed for the accomplishment of a considerable portion of the objectives for which they were undertaken; but they also occasioned a number of major temporary dislocations in the economic life of the country, including a near breakdown of the transportation system and a famine of serious dimensions. In the short term they weakened, rather than strengthened, the country's powers of military resistance.

We have already seen that Stalin was temperamentally inclined to look for security in a strengthening of the base of Soviet power at home, rather than in adventures of a revolutionary nature abroad. Now, as the dislocations produced by the hasty programs of industrialization and collectivization weakened the country's immediate

[1] Officially, the First Five Year Plan, shortened to four and a quarter years, ran from October 1, 1928, to December 31, 1932. It represented, of course, only the first phase of the program of industrialization which it inaugurated —a program in which the accent was predominantly on the military side.

military potential, the need for external peace became an urgent necessity of the country's situation.

Yet here there was a contradiction. If Stalin needed, on the one hand, the reality of peace, he also needed, as justification for the hardships and sufferings inflicted on the population, the appearance of acute external danger. He continued, therefore, throughout the period of the First Five Year Plan, to insist (*see Documents Nos. 23 and 24*) that the capitalist world had now entered upon another "cycle of wars and revolutions," comparable to that which had been experienced at the end of the First World War, and that this involved for Russia, once again, acute danger of foreign intervention and war.

The thesis of the new instability of capitalism found some sustenance, of course, in the world economic crisis which began in 1929. (*See Document No. 25.*) But even this did not prove that the capitalists were preparing for a new attack upon the Soviet Union. To lend greater credibility to this latter thesis, Stalin did not hesitate to stage, during the First Five Year Plan period, several mock trials and police actions, designed to suggest that foreign specialists and engineers employed in Russia were regularly engaged in all sorts of hostile acts of sabotage and subversion.[2] The impression these trials and incidents were meant to convey was that Russia was surrounded by enemies, and that it was foreign governments, not the Soviet government, that were responsible both for the hardships occasioned by the industrialization program and for the many evidences of bungling and inefficiency in its execution. This involved, of course, making

[2] These were, notably, the "Shakhty" trial of 1928, involving Germans and Poles; the "Industrial Party" trial of 1930, involving both French and British; and the arrest in 1933 of a group of engineers of the British Metropolitan-Vickers Company. The fraudulent nature of these trials was indicated by the fact that the leading victim of the "Industrial Party" trial Professor L. Ramzin, although formally condemned to 30 years confinement, appears actually to have continued his calling as a scientist in the years following his conviction. After the German attack in 1941, he was formally released and has subsequently taken normal part in Soviet scientific life. This lenience would never have been shown had he really been guilty of the offenses for which he was charged.

judicial scapegoats out of a number of foreigners who had been residing and working in the U.S.S.R., and thus abusing the foreign relations of the Soviet Union for domestic-political purposes. (*See Document No. 26.*)

Relations with the western countries were further strained at this time by the activities of the Comintern. Although not seriously attempting to produce immediate revolutions in any of the western countries, the communists lost no opportunity to exploit the economic crisis for the purpose of undermining confidence in western parliamentary institutions and of increasing their own influence.

Thus a competent Moscow observer of that day was able later, in describing Soviet policy during the First Five Year Plan period, to say that the Soviet Union "concealed an ironclad isolationism behind a façade of intensified Comintern activity which was designed in part to detract attention from her internal troubles." [3]

**The Establishment of Diplomatic Relations with the United States.** Throughout the period of Republican administrations in Washington, 1921 to 1933, the United States government had steadfastly refused to recognize the Soviet regime, citing as its reasons the responsibility of the Soviet leaders for the activities of the Comintern and their position in the matter of debts and claims. Franklin Roosevelt, when he became President in 1933, was relatively uninterested in these issues. He was, however, much worried about Japanese expansion in East Asia. He hoped, as did the Soviet leaders, that the existence of diplomatic contact between Russia and America might have a restraining effect upon the Japanese. Hitler's rise to power in Germany also no doubt appeared to him to increase the need for diplomatic contact with the Soviet government.

In the fall of 1933, therefore, at Roosevelt's invitation, the Soviet Foreign Commissar, Maxim Litvinov (who had replaced Chicherin in 1930), proceeded to Washington to discuss the resumption of relations. On November 16, 1933, notes were exchanged between the two

[3] This was the Counselor of the German Embassy in Moscow, Mr. Gustav Hilger. See Gustav Hilger and Alfred G. Meyer, *The Incompatible Allies* (New York, 1953), p. 225.

governments, establishing full diplomatic relations. They embodied a number of assurances from Litvinov as to the treatment the United States might expect to receive in individual questions, and as to Soviet policy in the matter of subversive propaganda.

American recognition (followed shortly by that of a number of other countries which had hitherto hung back) was regarded in Moscow as a triumph for Soviet diplomacy. (*See Document No. 27.*) It strengthened slightly the Soviet position vis-à-vis Japan. Insofar as it decreased Russia's international isolation, it could be regarded as at least a partial reply to the rise of Hitler. But its results were disappointing to both parties. While Roosevelt had indeed discussed with Litvinov the question of debts and claims prior to the act of recognition, the two men had failed to arrive at any real agreement on the subject. The President, like the British in 1924, now found the Soviet government even less inclined to make concessions in this matter once recognition had become a fact than they were before. The various public assurances which had been extracted from Litvinov at the time of recognition with regard to propaganda and other controversial matters proved, as State Department experts had forewarned, to be largely specious. Throughout the ensuing years down to the involvement of both powers in World War II, the Soviet-American relationship remained troubled, distant, and devoid of real political content.

**— Hitler's Accession to Power.** On January 30, 1933, the National-Socialist era was inaugurated in Germany with Adolf Hitler's accession to power in the position of Reichschancellor. In view of the violent antagonism to both domestic and foreign communism on which the Nazi program was based, and the key position which Germany had always occupied in Soviet policy, this event represented, of course, a major deterioration in the international position of the Soviet Union, particularly dangerous because it came on the very heels of the Japanese action in Manchuria.

One of the great controversial issues of Soviet foreign policy in the Thirties relates to Stalin's tardiness in reacting to this event. In the months preceding Hitler's accession to power, the German Communist Party was still a force to be reckoned with in German political life. In the elections of November 1932, it polled approximately six million votes. Together with the Social Democrats, it could have exerted a preponderant influence on political developments within Germany. Against the united opposition of communists and socialists, an assumption of power by the Nazis would scarcely have been possible. Yet throughout this period, the German communist leaders continued, under Moscow's orders, to pursue a course that greatly facilitated Hitler's success. This course consisted in treating their rivals in the socialist camp, the Social-Democrats, as the main enemy, and directing their energies primarily to the reduction of socialist strength rather than to combating the growing strength of the Nazis. So intense was the preoccupation of the German communist leaders with the struggle against their fellow socialists that they appear even to have viewed Hitler's advance to power with a certain complacency, hoping that Nazi brutality would serve to decimate the German Social-Democratic leadership and to drive the rank and file into the communist camp. There were even occasions when communist and Nazi actions appeared to go hand in hand. Not only did this policy, stubbornly continued under Comintern directives, facilitate Hitler's rise to power, but it proved disastrous to the German communists themselves, who were subsequently mercilessly slaughtered by Hitler's Gestapo.

**The Soviet Reaction to Hitler's Accession.** In the formal sense, Hitler's accession to office had no great immediate effect on German-Soviet relations. In May 1933, to be sure, the Soviet government abruptly canceled the clandestine military arrangements which had now endured with occasional vicissitudes since 1923. Otherwise Stalin exhibited nothing more than a desire to be left alone to pursue his domestic programs. Repeatedly, he caused the Germans to be assured that even the brutal measures of extermination now being taken against the German communists constituted no impediment, in his eyes, to a continuance of good relations between the two countries. Plainly, he hoped that the sharp edge of Nazi aggressiveness would in some way, without his doing, blunt itself against other objectives, leaving him free to pursue his internal programs without hindrance.

By the beginning of 1934, however, there were signs of a growing concern in Moscow over the attitudes and policies of the new German regime. The anticommunist utterances of the leading Nazis had not diminished in violence with their assumption of governmental power; and there had continued to be references to Russia, and particularly to the Ukraine, as predestined fields for German expansion. On more than one occasion, officials and employees of Soviet establishments in Germany had fallen foul of the Nazi persecution of Jews and socialists of all kinds. The abundant evidences of intent on Hitler's part to create a powerful German army constituted a basic alteration, and a most disturbing one, in the situation with which Russia was faced in Europe. A source of particular concern to Moscow must, one suspects, have been the Non-Aggression Pact concluded between Germany and Poland in January 1934. This agreement could only be taken as an indication that Hitler had turned his back on the Rapallo policy, aimed at a revision of Germany's eastern frontiers by agreement between Germany and Russia at the expense of Poland, and was now seeking to achieve such a revision by agreement with the Poles, at the ultimate expense of Russia. This, in the initial period of Hitler's power, was indeed the case.

**The Policy of Collective Security.** The realization of the extent to which Soviet security was being undermined by these developments produced, in early 1934, a change in Soviet policy which was to endure, on the surface at least, for a full four years. It was a policy aimed at stiffening the resistance of the western powers, particularly France and England, to Hitler, with a view either to frustrating his aggressive activities to such an extent as to cause him to lose prestige internally and to fall from power, or, if that could not be accomplished, to assuring that it would be the western powers, not Russia, who would bear the brunt of the resulting military conflict. This involved a dual effort: first, to persuade the French and British that it was they, not Russia, who were most endangered by Hitler's aggressive tendencies; secondly, to bind these powers to specific obligations of mutual military assistance, vis-à-vis the Soviet Union and other powers, which would assure that the weight of their influence and power would be fully enlisted as a restraint on Hitler's ambitions. These undertakings were pursued with great skill and persistence in the years 1934-1937 by Litvinov.

In pursuing this policy, the Soviet government was aided by the fact that Russia had no common border with Germany, whereas France, and in effect the other western democracies, did. This meant that in the case of a conflict with Germany which brought into operation such undertakings of mutual assistance, western forces might be expected to become immediately involved with the Germans in the initial stages of hostilities, whereas Russia, separated from Germany by a cordon of smaller eastern European states, would have time for hesitation and maneuver, and could choose the moment for the maximum commitment of her own strength. Thus the Soviet government could enter into such commitments with little fear of being forced in consequence to bear an undue share of the burden of an eventual military encounter with Germany. If the mere existence of such engagements sufficed to contain and frustrate the expansive force of Hitlerism, so much the better. If it did not, then the undertakings might provide at least *some* measure of insurance against the eventuality which was the nightmare of Soviet statesmanship: a war between Germany and Russia from which the western powers could remain aloof. (*See Document No. 28.*)

**Russia's Entrance into the League of Nations.** The effort to implement this policy took three main forms. One of these was the entrance of the Soviet Union into the League of Nations. Up to this time, the Soviet government had remained aloof from the League; and Soviet propagandists and statesmen had consistently denounced it as an instrument of the forces of imperialism. Now, in the light of the Nazi threat, this attitude changed. While no inordinate hopes were ever placed by the Soviet leaders on the effectiveness of the League as a hindrance to Hitler's ambitions, it was felt that the organization might, under Soviet encouragement, develop a certain supplementary usefulness in this respect, as well as with relation to the Japanese. In September 1934, with the help of the French, Russia's entry into the League was accomplished. The change was no doubt facilitated by the fact that Germany and Japan had only recently both withdrawn from the organization.

**The Franco-Soviet Pact.** Another major move undertaken by Moscow by way of implementation of the policy of collective security was the negotiation of mutual assistance pacts with France and Czechoslovakia. The motives which caused the Soviet government to pursue this objective with such persistence between 1934 and 1936 are somewhat obscure, for the French were already morally and politically obligated to come to the assistance of Czechoslovakia and Poland if either of these countries was attacked by the Germans; yet without invading them first, Hitler could scarcely have found a way to attack Russia on a broad front. Thus the pact could add little to France's existing obligations with relation to a possible military encounter in eastern Europe. One can only assume that Moscow saw its value primarily in its quality as a demonstration of solidarity in the light of the Nazi threat, and hoped that it would help to prevent a war from developing in the first instance.

The negotiations with the French over the conclusion of such a pact began in the winter and spring of 1934. They continued, with delays and interruptions, until May 2, 1935, when the pact was finally signed. Its ratification did not occur until March 1936. The companion pact with the Czechs, to which the Franco-Soviet Pact was linked, was signed on May 16, 1935, and ratified the following month.

**The Switch in Comintern Policy.** The third major facet of the Soviet quest for collective security was a change of policy in the Comintern, by virtue of which the communists in the western democratic countries were encouraged, belatedly, to restrain their internecine feuds with other socialists and to merge their efforts with those of liberal and democratic elements within their respective countries, with a view to creating a united front in resistance to the inroads of fascism both internally and externally. This change was first inaugurated in early 1934 in France, where right-wing elements, who would certainly have strongly opposed the policy of collective security, were already threatening to follow Hitler's example in the seizure of political leadership. The change of policy was given official sanction at the Seventh (and last) Comintern Congress, which was held in Moscow in the summer of 1935.

**Disillusionment with Collective Security.** Despite the vigor and scope of these efforts to restrain European fascism, the results were meager. In many capitals, and not least in London, there were serious inhibitions about any policy of collaboration with Soviet Russia, even for the containment of fascism. The League of Nations, reflecting these inhibitions, proved a feeble and ineffective reed. The final language of the Franco-Soviet Pact was complicated and vague, and its operation was made extensively contingent on prior action by the League of Nations. It was not followed up (until 1939, when it was much too late) by any concrete military discussions. The French government, finally, delayed so long with its ratification, and exhibited so many hesitations in the process, that its value as a political demonstration was reduced to almost negligible proportions. The contempt of the Germans for its existence was clearly demonstrated by the reoccupation of the Rhineland by the Germans, in March 1936; and the failure of the western powers to react with any strong measures showed how ineffective was the Pact for the purposes Moscow had had in mind in concluding it.

**The Spanish Civil War.** As for the last of the strings to the Soviet bow, the united front policy in Europe, this was the one which was last put to the crucial test. This test came in the form of the civil war that broke out in Spain in mid-July 1936.

With the origins of this conflict Moscow (contrary to the charges often levied against it) had nothing to do. Even when it had broken out, Stalin, with his characteristic caution and timidity, would have preferred to remain aloof. But this was not feasible. The immediate and energetic intervention of the Germans and Italians[4] meant that if Russia failed to intervene, an early and dramatic victory of the insurgents could hardly be avoided. Such a victory would have meant the encirclement of France by the fascists, the probable triumph of fascist

[4] There is no question but that Franco had military aid from the Italians even before launching the uprising.

tendencies within France herself, and the further weakening of western resistance to Hitler. The way would then be clear for a German aggression toward the East.

After some initial hesitation, the Soviet leaders decided, in early September 1936, to intervene incisively in the Spanish situation. Having made this decision, they pressed the action forward with extraordinary speed and energy. Up to that time, there had not even been any Soviet official representation in Spain. By the end of November, Moscow had hundreds of advisers there; Soviet military supplies were already en route in major quantities; Soviet agents were in complete charge of military operations on the Madrid front. Within the space of a few months Moscow had gained effective control over large and crucial segments both of the Spanish-Republican military effort and of the normal functions of the Spanish government. Secret police, counterintelligence, censorship, propaganda, cryptographic procedures, the system of political commissars throughout the armed forces and the actual command of the Spanish-Republican air force: all these were the provinces of Moscow-directed communist agents. The Soviet military commanders and advisers, who supplied all the tanks and the larger part of the aircraft used on the Republican side, even maintained their own tank depots and military airfields, to which the Spanish government had no normal access and about which it was not even regularly informed.

The Spanish-Republican government did not particularly relish this wholly inordinate role of the Soviet Union in Spanish affairs. But Russia was at that time the only outside force giving aid in appreciable quantities; and Moscow ably exploited this fact.

There is no question but that this communist stiffening of the Republican military effort enabled Madrid to hold out against the initial attack by Franco and the military party in the fall of 1936 and thus prevented a speedy and spectacular victory of the insurgents. However, German and Italian intervention soon assumed such dimensions that it became clear by early 1937 that the final rescue of the Republic would be possible only by dint of much larger volume of assistance than Moscow had yet been able to give. The western democracies showed no evidence of any desire to provide even a portion of this assistance. Russia herself was poorly placed to give it; and for her to make the effort alone would have been to incur a heavy, overt commitment, extensively engaging her prestige, and possibly involving her in a war with the Axis.

Early in 1937, therefore, the Soviet government evidently reconciled itself to eventual defeat of the Republican cause; and its aid began to taper off. Its efforts from that time on were designed primarily to prolong the struggle, so that Spain would continue to draw off German and Italian energies for as long as possible. So long as the Axis was committed there, Stalin felt that he had a certain precarious immunity from German attack.

Such military aid as Moscow gave to the Republican side was given clandestinely. Initially, just before its decision to intervene, the Soviet government had reluctantly adhered (August 5, 1936) to the international agreement, pressed by the British, for nonintervention in Spanish affairs. Soon thereafter, however, having decided to send aid and "advisers," it took pains to qualify this adherence (October 23) by the statement that it could not consider itself bound by this agreement "to any greater extent than any of the other participants." Since the Italians, in particular, were violating it right and left, and continued to do so throughout most of the war, this formally freed Moscow's hands. The laxity of the British and French in winking at Italian and German evasions of the nonintervention agreement was a source of bitter reproach in Moscow. It became one more leading item in the bill of indictment Litvinov was constantly levying against the western democracies for their failure to "stand up" to fascism. (*See Document No. 29.*)

As the civil war progressed, Spain became in increasing measure a theater of the internecine political struggle between Stalin and the anti-Stalin factions within the world socialist movement. Aware of the fact that the Spanish conflict was becoming a focal point and symbol for socialist and liberal sentiment throughout the world, Stalin was evidently apprehensive lest the Republican cause in Spain become dominated by his rivals and enemies within the socialist camp. This would have strengthened the hands of the opposition to him within Russia, and would have embarrassed him in his control of the Comintern. From the beginning of 1937, therefore, a considerable part of the Soviet effort in Spain was directed to the destruction of the anti-Stalinist factions within the Spanish socialist and anarchist movements, and to the maintenance of a virtual monopoly of control over the international volunteer element fighting on the Republican side. In both of these efforts the Soviet control over the Spanish secret police was employed ruthlessly and to good effect. But this exploitation of Soviet influence in Spain for what were, in effect, domestic-political purposes of the Stalin regime caused, as time went on, a growing resentment in Spanish-Republican circles, and did much to nullify the psychological effects of Soviet aid. There were, in particular, instances where the demands of Stalin's vendetta against rival socialist groups conflicted with the demands of the war effort of the Republic. When this happened, precedence was given quite ruthlessly by the Kremlin to the first of these two requirements, to the embitterment of the Spanish Republican leaders.

**The Purges.** It is noteworthy that the Spanish civil war coincided almost exactly with the high point of the Soviet purges of the late Thirties, by means of which Stalin contrived to disembarrass himself not only of those senior figures within the Party who had opposed him politically on past occasions but also of a major portion of the senior officialdom, civilian and military, of the country. This extraordinary series of persecutions, in the course of which tens of thousands of faithful servants of the Soviet state were executed or consigned to death in penal camps on the basis of forced confessions and rigged procedures of one sort or another, was of so savage and undiscriminating a character, and did such serious damage both to the Soviet state and to the morale of the Party, that it is difficult to believe that it was the work of a wholly normal mind. It was something that could have occurred, in any case, only in the fevered and unreal atmosphere of a full-fledged totalitarian state.

It is difficult to determine to what extent the purges were connected with questions of foreign policy. The confessions of the defendants in the major "show" trials to various plottings and iniquities on behalf of foreign governments were untrustworthy and largely implausible, and provide no clew. That Stalin suffered reproach at the hands of the Opposition in 1933-1934, both for the sorry state to which the country had been reduced by the Five Year Plan and collectivization, and for his initial underestimation of the Nazi danger, seems clear. One cannot help noting that it was just at this time that the purges had their origin. Their most extreme and morbid phase, however, was inaugurated in the early summer of 1936. By September this had plainly led to a major crisis within the Party. The decision to intervene militarily in the Spanish civil war coincided almost to the day with the high point of this internal Party crisis. Many people have been struck, too, with the fact that scarcely one of the Soviet agents, military or civilian, who served in Spain escaped the long arm of Stalin's cruelty. Many were abruptly recalled to Russia in the midst of what was undoubtedly an earnest and even dedicated performance of their duties in Spain, never to be heard from again. Others were murdered in Spain or elsewhere abroad by punitive squads sent out expressly for the purpose. The few who escaped at the time seem to have suffered special persecution later. Was a particular savagery manifested toward those who served in Spain, or was the explanation simply that these were people who would normally have fallen foul of the purges anyway, but whose disappearances were merely the more conspicuous for the fact that they were abroad and in contact with foreigners when the blow fell?

To these questions there is, as yet, no reliable answer. It must have been clear to Stalin, by mid-1936, that the policy of collective security was failing, and that, as things were going, it would only be a matter of time before he would be faced with a choice of taking Hitler on in a military encounter or of finding some way to buy him off. In either case, he would need maximum freedom of action, and maximum freedom from criticism and interference by an embittered opposition which had always questioned his conduct of foreign policy. These reflections might, of course, have influenced his decision to launch the final and most violent phase of the purges. But the best evidence would suggest that the timing of this decision was occasioned primarily by internal factors (notably the stage reached in his effort to turn the secret police into a pliant and reliable agency of his personal power), and that its close correspondence in time with the decision to intervene in Spain was largely coincidental.

One thing, however, is now clear. The purges did result in a serious weakening of the Soviet military establishment. In this way, they had a good deal to do with the poor performance of the Red Army in the war with Finland (1939-1940) and in the initial stages of Russia's participation in World War II. This weakening of the military potential came at a time when the Soviet Union had the most urgent need for a rapid development of its defense capacity. It is difficult to believe that a series of measures which had this effect could have had their origins in considerations of foreign policy.

# — 8 —

# THE GERMAN-SOVIET NONAGGRESSION PACT

**The Year 1937.** We have seen that by the middle of 1936 the Soviet government had become seriously concerned over the meager prospects of the policy of "collective security." If the western democracies could not be induced to challenge Hitler over such issues as the German reoccupation of the Rhineland and the help given to the insurgents in Spain, what hope was there? The Rhineland was, after all, Hitler's last major demand against the western powers. His remaining known desiderata—Austria, the Sudeten-German portions of Czechoslovakia, Memel, Danzig, the Polish Corridor—all lay to the East. The next Nazi aggression, plainly, would be eastward, toward the Soviet borders. Russia was now in the danger zone. The progress of German rearmament suggested that she might have two or three years of grace, not more.

We have already noted that it was at this point that the purges began in earnest. Their most acute phase lasted for roughly two years—to the summer of 1938. In the show-trials and denunciations by which they were punctuated, every effort was made once again to portray the hostile world of capitalism as the root of all evil. The senior purge victims were generally depicted as "spies, wreckers and diversionists," inspired and directed by foreign governments.

Astute foreign observers in Moscow noticed that in this reaffirmation of the time-honored thesis of the hostility of the outside world, no distinction was being made between the fascist countries and the democracies, between the "aggressive" and the "peaceful" states. During the high period of "collective security" this distinction had stood at the center of the Soviet foreign policy line. Now, in 1937 and 1938, this line continued, to be sure, to be put forward by Litvinov for foreign consumption; but at home, in the internal party line interpreting the purges, the distinction was dropped. When, in early 1938, the Soviet government proceeded (in some unfathomable connection with the purges) to insist on the removal of most of the foreign consulates from Soviet cities, not only was no distinction made between those of Germany, Italy, and Japan, on the one hand, and those of the western democracies, on the other, but the matter was deliberately handled in such a way as to convey the impression that the closing of the British consulate in Leningrad was a measure forced upon a reluctant Litvinov by the pressure of an indignant public opinion, aroused by the revelations of the purges. This was a plain hint that the policy of collective security was under fire from powerful elements in the Party, who preferred to see no distinction, from the standpoint of Soviet interests, between the democracies and the fascist governments of western Europe.

During the year 1937 the purges evidently absorbed a great deal of the attention of the Soviet leaders. Aside from the preoccupation with the Spanish civil war (where Soviet policy was, from early 1937, one of gradual retirement), Stalin's main concern in external policy at that time appears to have been to gain maximum independence and freedom of maneuver. To this end he wished, particularly, to "normalize" Soviet relations with Germany. This desire had, in fact, never been absent at any time from his calculations. The deterioration in German-Soviet relations had from the beginning been Hitler's choice, not his. But now, with the patent failure of the only possible alternative—the policy of "collective security"—the incentive to such a normalization had become greater than ever.

**Effect of the Reunion of Austria and Germany.** The German annexation of Austria, in the spring of 1938, and the increased pressure on Czechoslovakia by which it was shortly followed, caused new alarm in Moscow and added a new note of urgency to the need for a restoration of the bond to Berlin. It is not surprising, therefore, that the first six months of 1938 were marked, on the one hand, by a number of cryptic warnings to the western powers that if they failed to take advantage of Moscow's willingness to collaborate in the organization of collective security, it might soon be too late, and, on the other hand, by new and stronger hints to Berlin that a normalization of German-Soviet relations would not be unwelcome in Moscow. In late May, 1938, the new Soviet ambassador to Berlin, A. T. Merekalov, arrived in Berlin with instructions to press the development of German-Soviet commercial relations.[1] A few days later, the Moscow press censor, after long and careful deliberation, passed for publication abroad a story by a foreign correspondent to the effect that Moscow would soon be approaching Berlin for an improvement in relations.[2] Immediately thereafter a major speech delivered by Litvinov, review-

[1] Merekalov's predecessor, Jacob Surits, was Jewish; and it was clear that he could not be a vehicle for negotiation with the violently anti-Semitic Nazis. After Surits' removal, the post had remained vacant for more than a year. The fact that the post was now filled, and filled by a non-Jew, was in itself a significant gesture.

[2] See Telegram, June 22, 1938, from the American Chargé d'Affaires at Moscow to the Secretary of State, *Foreign Relations of the United States, Diplomatic Papers: The Soviet Union, 1933-1939* (Washington, 1952), pp. 584-585.

ing and reaffirming the Soviet Union's policy of collective security, failed to appear at all in the Moscow press, though it was released for publication abroad.

Each of these developments, in itself of minor significance, was a straw in the wind; together, their significance was unmistakable. Nor were they entirely without reciprocal effect. Hitler was at that time still far from thinking of a deal with Russia. But his own situation was now becoming more delicate. He, too, now needed greater latitude of maneuver. The German government was therefore not averse to a moderate reduction of the tension. In July 1938 an oral agreement was arrived at between the Soviet government and the German ambassador in Moscow for a mutual cessation of press abuse of the respective heads of states. This was followed a few weeks later by a similar agreement on the cessation of press polemics generally.

**The Munich Crisis.** It is not likely that Stalin already had in mind, in the early months of 1938, anything so definite and drastic as the partition of eastern Europe between Russia and Germany which was later to be realized. He had as yet no firm plan of action. He, like Hitler, was concerned primarily to assure himself of maximum freedom of maneuver in what now loomed ahead as a dangerous and crucial period in world affairs. But the Munich settlement, occurring at the end of September 1938, created a new situation.

As the Nazi pressure on Czechoslovakia reached its climax in the month of September, the Soviet government, alone among the great powers, expressed its readiness to come to Czechoslovakia's defense if the Germans attacked—provided the French did likewise,[3] and provided, also, of course, that the Czechs themselves chose to fight. This gesture represented the last fling of the collective security policy in which Litvinov had invested so much effort.

Actually, Moscow risked little in taking this position. The Polish and Rumanian governments were known to

[3] This was in strict accord with the letter of the Soviet-Czechoslovak Treaty of Mutual Assistance of May 16, 1935, which obliged the U.S.S.R. to come to the assistance of Czechoslovakia only in the event that France did the same.

be averse to any passage of Soviet troops across their territory. Yet without crossing the territory of one of these states it was impossible for Soviet troops to reach Czechoslovakia at all. Even had this political impediment not existed, railway and road connections between Russia and western Czechoslovakia were so awkward and primitive that many weeks would have had to elapse before even so much as a single Soviet division could have been moved to the Bohemian area. Soviet assistance, therefore, would in any event have been necessarily confined, in the initial (and in this instance crucial) period of hostilities, to some air support and a few advisers, à la Spain. But, contrasting as it did with the hesitations of the French and British governments, the Soviet gesture at the time of Munich made a deep and lasting impression on liberal opinion in the West. To many people in the western democracies, distressed by the weakness of their own government's reaction, it seemed that only the Soviet government had shown both political realism and loyalty to its obligations at this crucial juncture.

Despite his immediate triumph at Munich, Hitler found his own situation even more complicated by the consequences of the settlement. He was unhappily impressed by the sharp criticism and questioning to which Chamberlain's policy was subjected in the wake of the Munich conference. Resolved in his own mind to "solve the Polish question" within the space of a year, he was obliged to recognize that Munich had lessened rather than strengthened the chances that England and France could be brought to remain aloof in the event of a German action against Poland.

In these circumstances, his mind appears to have turned first, as it had turned in 1934, to the possibility of a deal with the Polish government itself by which Poland would voluntarily satisfy German aspirations relating to her western frontier, in return for German support for Poland's ambitions in the area of the Ukraine. In the first weeks of 1939, German diplomacy was directed to this end. But whereas in 1934 the German-Polish agreement had implied for Poland only an implicit obligation not to combine with Russia in opposing Hitler, such an agreement now clearly implied the voluntary relinquishment by Poland of Danzig, large parts of the Corridor, and other border areas as well. To this, to Hitler's intense irritation, the Poles now demurred. Throughout the winter of 1938-1939, the Germans had respected, partly out of consideration for Polish feelings, the obligation, implicit in the Munich settlement, not to occupy the remainder of Czechoslovakia. Now, in the light of Polish recalcitrance, Hitler changed his mind. In mid-March 1939, the German forces occupied the remainder of Bohemia and Moravia, turning large parts of Ruthenia and Slovakia over to the Hungarians, thus wholly extinguishing the Czechoslovak state. This act of flagrant bad faith (followed one week later by Lithuania's forced concession of the Memel district to Germany) caused the cup of British and French patience to overflow. It brought London and Paris to the realization that any further attempt on Hitler's part to expand his domination by force of arms could be successfully opposed only by major war. Within the month following the German entry into Prague, both Britain and France gave formal guarantees against aggression to both Poland and Rumania.

**The German-Soviet Rapprochement.** For Hitler's eastern policy these guarantees, particularly the British guarantee to Poland, were decisive. They made it evident that barring the contingency of a successful German deal with Russia, an attack on Poland would mean war with the West. The neutralization of Russia now became a matter of urgent importance in German policy.

In the early winter of 1939, Hitler, evidently believing that this would facilitate his talks with the Poles, had abruptly canceled certain arrangements agreed upon in December 1938 for negotiations in Moscow looking toward a new German-Soviet credit agreement. His action in doing so had come as a new blow to Soviet hopes for a German-Soviet rapprochement. But Stalin, though suspicious and discouraged, did not abandon his efforts in this direction. On March 10, at the XVIII Party Congress, he delivered a speech (*see Document No. 30*) in which he made it abundantly clear that the Soviet Union did not propose to become involved in a war with Hitler for the benefit of the western powers. He enjoined the policy makers of the Communist Party, among other things, "to be cautious and not allow our country to be drawn into conflict by warmongers who are accustomed to have others pull the chestnuts out of the fire for them. . . ."

This speech was meant as the clearest sort of hint to the Germans that Russia was ready to come to a deal with them, by which she would purchase, at the expense of Poland, her own immunity from attack.[4] If Hitler understood this, he gave no sign at the moment. But on April 28, in a major speech on foreign affairs, he denounced the 1934 pact with Poland, and carefully refrained from mentioning in any way the Soviet Union. The significance of this omission was not lost on Stalin. One week later, Litvinov was abruptly removed from his office as People's Commissar for Foreign Affairs and Molotov, then Soviet Premier, was appointed in his place. For the first time since Trotsky laid down the office in the middle of the Brest-Litovsk crisis in 1918, Russian diplomacy was now to be conducted personally by a member of the all-powerful Politburo. This was a sure sign, first, that Moscow was turning its back on Litvinov's efforts toward "collective security"; and, secondly, that it was preparing itself for major diplomatic negotiations.

Hitler, who had heretofore been skeptical of the good faith of Soviet gestures toward better relations, now became seriously interested. But an attempt by the Germans in mid-May to revive the credit talks, still unresumed after Hitler's action of late January, brought the response from Molotov that the talks could be renewed only when a "political basis" for them had been provided. This statement, meant from the Soviet side as a favorable hint, was taken by Hitler as a rebuff. This delayed the progress of the rapprochement for another two months.

**Fighting on the Mongolian Border.** During these weeks of May and June, Soviet spokesmen continued to indicate to the Germans the interest of their government in an agreement. Their anxiety to avoid war in Europe was unquestionably heightened, just at this time, by the situation on the borders of the Russian Far East and Mongolia. In the preceding summer, military encounters on a serious scale had taken place between

[4] For the fact that this was intended as a hint we have the authority of Stalin himself, who later told Ribbentrop with pride that he meant it exactly this way.

Soviet and Japanese forces in the vicinity of the conjunction of the Manchurian, Korean, and Siberian borders. Then, in the summer of 1939, Japanese forces became embroiled with Soviet and Soviet-Mongolian forces along the border between Manchuria and Outer Mongolia. The initiative in provoking these clashes lay unquestionably with the Japanese, who were evidently concerned to probe Soviet strength and the seriousness of the repeated Soviet declarations that Siberian and Outer Mongolian territory would be defended. The battle which developed in the summer of 1939 assumed the proportions of full-scale warfare, involving the use of entire divisions and of tanks and airplanes running into the hundreds. Although the Soviet forces appear to have come out best in this test of strength, defending successfully the borders to which they were committed, the scale of the hostilities was such as to cause acute concern to the Soviet government, and to intensify its desire to purchase immunity from involvement in any European conflict just at that time.

**Negotiations with the British and French.** Meanwhile, the situation as between the Germans and the Russians was complicated by negotiations which had been entered into by the Soviet government with the British and French governments, looking to the conclusion of a mutual assistance pact between the three powers and to the issuance of a joint guarantee to a number of countries thought to be in danger of German attack. Exchanges on these subjects were begun through diplomatic channels as early as mid-April, in connection with the British guarantee to Poland. Formal negotiations were pursued in Moscow from early June until the middle of August. Stalin and Molotov, in stringing along these negotiations with the French and British throughout the summer, used them without scruple as a means of putting pressure on the Germans. At the same time, they successfully concealed from the French and British negotiators the fact that parallel talks with the Germans were in progress.

Up to approximately the early part of July, Hitler, though already resolved on Poland's eventual destruction, appears still to have toyed with the idea of contenting himself in 1939 with a limited action to achieve Danzig's re-incorporation into the Reich. He evidently still hoped, at that time, that this objective, which would satisfy his need for a new political triumph before autumn, could be achieved in such a way as not to provoke a general European war. At some time in early July, however, he appears to have abandoned this scheme and to have resolved finally on the general attack against Poland, to be launched at the end of August. Military planning for such an attack had long been under way. Now the actual military measures looking to its execution were at once put in hand. Evidences of them were plainly visible to foreign intelligence services by the end of July.

Once the decision had been taken to attack Poland on a broad front in the face of Anglo-French guarantees to Poland, the achievement of a deal with Russia, as a means of avoiding a two-front war, now became a matter of great urgency for Hitler. German hesitations with regard to both political and economic negotiations with Russia now disappeared. The trade talks were resumed in mid-July. Before the end of the month German representatives were pressing hard, in private talks with their Soviet counterparts, for an agreement which would give Russia immunity from involvement in the impending war, in return for her promise not to interfere.

It was now the Russians' turn to be suspicious. For some days Molotov and Stalin hung back, looking for a trap. They suspected that the Germans were pursuing the talks with Moscow only in order to drive a better bargain, themselves, with the British and French. They continued to string along the unsuspecting British and French negotiators, who had now been joined by military representatives. But their hand was forced on August 15, when the Germans launched a thunderbolt in the form of a proposal to send the German Foreign Minister, von Ribbentrop, to Moscow in the near future "to set forth the Führer's views to Herr Stalin" and "to lay the foundation for a definite improvement in German-Soviet relations." [5] Pointedly, it was explained in the German mes-

[5] *Nazi-Soviet Relations, 1939-1941: Documents from the Archives of the German Foreign Office,* edited by Raymond James Sontag and James Stuart Beddie (Department of State, 1948), pp. 50-52.

sage that the Polish-German crisis made "a speedy clarification of German-Russian relations desirable." This was followed, the next day, August 16, by a further message asking that the date for Ribbentrop's arrival be advanced to August 18, on the grounds that "in view of the present situation, and of the possibility of the occurrence any day of serious incidents . . . , a basic and rapid clarification of German-Russian relations and the mutual adjustment of the pressing questions are desirable." [6]

Stalin was now definitely on the spot. It was clear from a number of indications, including the wording of these German communications, that war between Germany and Poland would begin within a matter of days. It was true that the western powers had guaranteed Polish independence, and showed signs of a readiness to enter into a state of war with Germany in the event of an attack on Poland. But would they really fight? If they hung back, as at Munich, or if, having declared war, they failed to pursue vigorous offensive operations, Hitler's forces might soon appear on the Soviet border. The only way of obviating this danger was to make a deal with Hitler that would have the effect of keeping the Germans at a distance.

In the final military negotiations with the British and French, the Soviet negotiators had pressed the western governments to obtain assurances from the Poles and Rumanians that they would admit Soviet forces to their territory in the event Russia should ally herself with the western democracies. They had also pressed hard, throughout the negotiations, for what amounted in effect to British and French agreement that Russia should be free to enter and occupy the Baltic States (Latvia, Lithuania, and Estonia) in case their neutrality appeared in Soviet eyes to be compromised. Had Stalin received satisfaction on these demands, and had the deal with the French and British then matured, his intention undoubtedly was to occupy as much as he could of these countries as a countermove to a German entry into Poland. This, too, to the extent it was successful, would have served the purpose of keeping the Germans at a distance.

[6] *Ibid.*, p. 58.

But the Poles and Rumanians had been adamant in their refusal to permit passage of Russian troops, believing that the latter, once admitted, would never leave. And the British and French had shown themselves unwilling to sign what amounted to an abandonment of the Baltic States to Stalin's mercies. The Germans, on the other hand, had been hinting plainly, since mid-July, at a partition of eastern Europe, as part of the price to be paid for Russian neutrality. They had indicated that they might be willing to leave the Baltic States, and perhaps even a portion of Poland, on the Soviet side of the line.

The situation, then, boiled down to this: with war now inevitable in eastern Europe, Stalin was determined to acquire a "glacis," or buffer zone, there which would at least keep the German forces at a distance from the existing Soviet borders. Forced to define this *glacis* in geographic terms, he named those areas of the old Tsarist empire (the Baltic States, eastern Poland, and a portion of Rumania) which had been lost to Russia at the time of the revolution. In addition to gaining him space which, in the event of a later German-Russian conflict, he could trade for time, this acquisition, by restoring Russia's pre-war western frontier, would wipe out the shame of the Brest-Litovsk settlement and contribute greatly to his own prestige. Faced with the choice between *opposing* Hitler on the strength of an alliance with the British and French, who were unwilling to hand these areas over to him as a price for his participation in the war, or keeping aloof from the war on the strength of a deal with Hitler, who had no compunction at throwing these areas (for the moment, at least) in as part of the bargain, Stalin chose for Hitler.

The proposal for Ribbentrop's visit was therefore accepted. Although it could not be arranged on two days' notice, as the Germans had requested, it was fixed for August 23, and Ribbentrop arrived on that day. Within the space of twenty-four hours, agreement was reached on a Nonaggression Pact supplemented by a secret Protocol, dividing eastern Europe into "spheres of influence." (*See Document No. 31.*) Although it was not stipulated what each side should do within its allotted sphere of influence, both sides understood very well, in arriving at this agreement, that they were removing the last barrier to the outbreak of hostilities, that Germany and Poland would be at war within a fortnight, and that the agreement they were concluding would mean the end of Polish independence.

# — 9 —

# THE FAILURE OF THE NONAGGRESSION PACT

**The War and the Partition of Poland.** Almost eight days, to the hour, after the signature of the German-Soviet Pact in Moscow, the German armies struck along the Polish frontier. One week later, they were at the gates of Warsaw. A further fortnight saw the crushing of the last serious military resistance on the part of the Poles. Meanwhile, on September 3, Britain and France had declared war on Germany.

For Moscow, this precipitate course of events created a new, unexpected, and in many ways disturbing situation. The Soviet leaders, betrayed by their memories of Munich and failing to realize the change that had come over western opinion, had hardly expected that the British and French would really go to war. The German-Soviet Nonaggression Pact, they had thought, would remove whatever disposition there was in London and Paris to honor the guarantee to Poland. Now, instead of the limited German-Polish encounter with regard to which they had endeavored to protect their interests, they found themselves confronted with a full-fledged European war. This had advantages: the pleasing dream of an embroilment of the western powers with Hitler in an encounter from which Russia could remain aloof seemed now, unexpectedly, to have come closer. Yet the very existence of a general European war spelled greatly heightened danger for the Soviet Union, particularly in view of the poor state of readiness of the Soviet armed forces in the wake of the destructive purges. Besides, when it came to actual military operations, the western powers were remaining ominously passive on the western front; and the Germans were doing the same. Only in the east was fighting in progress; and here the speed and scope of the German advance was surpassing everything Moscow had anticipated. By mid-September, the German armies had already swept into large sections of the territory allotted to the Soviet "sphere of influence" by the accord of August 23. The Soviet leaders were obliged, therefore, to move much more hastily than they had anticipated, in order to protect the interests they had staked out in the agreement with the Germans.

On September 17 the Soviet armed forces crossed the Polish border and proceeded to occupy the allotted Soviet "sphere of influence," the Germans loyally retiring to make way for them. The pretext put forward publicly was a shabby one. Not being in a position to mention the secret protocol, on the basis of which this action was actually taken, and lacking any more impressive pretext, the Soviet government found no better public justification for the move than the racial affinity of a portion of the people in the affected Polish districts with peoples in the Soviet Union. It depicted its action as the fulfillment of a "sacred duty" to take under Soviet protection the "kindred Ukrainians and White [Byelo-] Russians" of this region. (*See Document No. 32.*)

The stress of these events demonstrated the need for a clearer and more detailed arrangement for Poland's partition than the one that had been so hastily concocted on the night of August 23-24. Ribbentrop was consequently obliged to make another journey to Moscow at the end of September (September 27 to 29) for the purpose of negotiating a supplementary agreement. This new settlement clarified, and somewhat altered, the terms of the division of eastern Europe. The new line of division followed roughly the ethnic lines, the Germans getting practically all of the purely Polish territory, the Soviet Union getting the Byelo-Russian and Ukrainian districts adjacent to the old Soviet frontier. Lithuania, which in the August agreement had been assigned to the

German sphere, was now also, on Soviet insistence, allotted to the Soviet sphere. (*See Document No. 33.*) Plainly, Moscow was now stepping up the price for its neutrality, in view of the fact that the British and French governments had, contrary to the expectations of both parties in August, actually gone to war.

Had the Soviet government, in taking over these areas which had for two decades been included in the Polish state, acted with humanity and tolerance in its treatment of the inhabitants, a good case could have been made for the thesis that its action had been no more than a legitimate and unavoidable defense of the traditional and geographic interests of the Russian state, in the face of the menace of Hitlerism. Unfortunately, in the ensuing months the Soviet authorities proceeded, with great ruthlessness and cruelty, to disperse or destroy those people in the newly acquired regions who, because of their "bourgeois" origin, their patriotic Polish disposition, their previous governmental connections, or even, in some instances, because of the respect and affection in which they were held by neighbors, were ideologically unacceptable to Moscow or were considered to present a potential problem to the consolidation of Soviet rule. Within a few months some hundreds of thousands of such people,[1] the overwhelming majority of them quite guiltless of any specific resistance to, or offense against, Soviet authority, were arrested and deported to Siberia or other remote regions of the Soviet Union. The means by which this operation was conducted were so cruel that scarcely one-half of the victims are believed to have survived both the deportation and the subsequent hardships of wartime exile. By these and other acts of gratuitous cruelty, the Soviet Union forfeited whatever merit it could have claimed for its acquisition of eastern Poland, and laid the groundwork for the policies destined to be pursued in the satellite area in the aftermath of World War II. The same must unhappily be said for the Soviet treatment of the population in the other eastern European territories acquired by the Soviet Union in the period of 1939-1940.

[1] The widely varying estimates of their number seem to center around the figure of one million.

**The Baltic States.** In addition to occupying eastern Poland, the Soviet government lost no time in exploiting the German concession that the three Baltic countries of Latvia, Estonia, and Lithuania should fall to the Russian sphere of influence. Simultaneously with the move into Poland, Soviet forces were massed on the frontiers of the Baltic States. Beginning September 25, peremptory demands were made on the Baltic governments to sign mutual assistance pacts which would permit the stationing of Soviet garrisons and bases on their territory. Cut off, militarily, from the West, and sold out politically by Germany, the three governments yielded without resistance. The last of the three pacts (that with Lithuania) was signed on October 10. By this move the respective countries were reduced, for the time being, to the status of protectorates, retaining their own governments and the integrity of their internal administration. This change, as will be seen, was the prologue to an early end of their national independence.

**Finland.** In the case of Finland, the Soviet government had already been endeavoring, since April 1938, to persuade the Finnish government to grant to the Soviet Union facilities for a naval base somewhere near the middle or the mouth of the Gulf of Finland, either on the Finnish coast or adjacent islands, and to agree to a corrective of the frontier on the outskirts of Leningrad, designed to give more room for a possible defense of the city by Soviet forces. From the strictly military standpoint, and assuming that they concealed no improper political motives, these requests were not unreasonable. The Finns, however, were suspicious. Up to the outbreak of the European war they rigorously rejected all Russian proposals of this nature.

Now that Finland had been assigned to the Soviet sphere of influence (in the first German-Soviet agreement) and German support for Finland was no longer to be feared, Soviet leaders set out to crack this nut as well. Finnish negotiators were summoned to Moscow at the beginning of October, simultaneously with the placing of pressure on the Baltic States. On October 11 negotiations were begun, with Stalin's personal participation. Again, the Finns proved completely adamant. The talks ended, unsuccessfully, on November 11, the Russians making it quite clear that they would, in the event of continued Finnish recalcitrance, use force.

The Soviet demands, even at this late date, were neither unreasonable nor inflexible; and there were moderate Finns who felt that the Finnish government should have attempted to meet them halfway, particularly since the Russians showed themselves relatively patient and moderate in the negotiations. But by this time the Finns had before them the example of Moscow's cavalier treatment of the other Baltic governments; and their reluctance to enter on a path of concessions to which there seemed to be no visible and reassuring end is not difficult to understand.

Less than three weeks after the breakdown of the talks, Soviet forces attacked Finland, thus inaugurating what was known as the Winter War. Because the Soviet command underestimated the Finnish strength and launched the operation with inadequate forces, the Finns at first scored a number of spectacular successes. But when the Russians had recovered from these initial mistakes, their superiority in sheer mass began to tell. By late February, although the Soviet had not yet advanced deeply into Finland, the Finnish cause had become militarily hopeless. In March, the Finns were obliged to accept Soviet terms, and the fighting ended.

**Soviet Reaction to Developments in the West.** Meanwhile, opinion in the western democracies, moved by the brutality of the Soviet attack on Finland and the heroism of Finnish resistance, had rallied strongly to the Finnish side. There was much talk, over the winter months, of the possible despatch of Allied expeditions to the relief of the Finns—a move which, as it happened, would also have served the Allied war effort against Germany by giving the Allies control of the important iron ore fields in northern Sweden. The Finnish capitulation put an end, of course, to the talk of such an expedition. But the British went ahead to occupy themselves throughout the remainder of March with plans to mine Norwegian territorial waters and, in the event of German counteraction, to secure certain Norwegian ports. These plans the Germans proceeded to anticipate by their move into Denmark and Norway on April 9.

Throughout the final weeks before the German move

into Scandinavia, there were signs of much uneasiness in Moscow. The prospect of a British force appearing on the Finnish border, as the friend of the Finns, did not fit at all with Stalin's determination to remain aloof from the war. For a time, the Germans found themselves treated with cold reserve in Moscow. But the successful German move against Norway and Denmark put an end to these hesitations. Now that Germany had firmly inserted its power between England and Finland, Moscow's worries were relieved. The Germans were at once congratulated by Molotov on the success of their operation, and the outward cordiality of the German-Soviet relationship was for the time being restored.

By the same token, the German move against France and the Low Countries in mid-May was also initially welcomed in Moscow, where it was assumed that this marked the beginning of a long and mutually exhausting military encounter between the Germans and the western powers, from which Russia could remain aloof.[2] But again, the unexpectedly rapid success of the German operations disturbed this pleasing prospect. Beneath the surface little confidence was wasted between Hitler and Stalin; and it was only too apparent in Moscow that an easy and rapid German victory in the West could undermine the foundation on which the Nonaggression Pact had been concluded. This would free Hitler's hands to pursue a policy in the East more closely attuned to his own anticommunist convictions.

It was only Britain's refusal to admit defeat, and the unpreparedness of the Germans to launch an invasion of England in 1940, which prevented this danger from arising for Moscow in its full ugliness. But the nearness of the danger, particularly in May and June of 1940, caused Stalin to take advantage of the apparent favorable moment and to proceed, with what seems today to have been ill-considered haste and greed, to realize the remainder of the assets which he considered to have accrued to the Soviet Union, implicitly or explicitly, by virtue of the pacts of August and September 1939. He therefore moved (June 1940), with only scant and late notice to the Germans, to extinguish the quasi-autonomy

[2] Again, Molotov congratulated the Germans on the fall of Paris.

which had been left to the Baltic States and to incorporate these countries entirely into the Soviet Union. This procedure was conducted with such cynical ruthlessness and abruptness, and in a manner so contemptuous of the national feelings of the respective peoples, that it again cost the Soviet Union heavily in terms of the loss of confidence and sympathy throughout the world. At the same time, the Soviet government presented an ultimatum to Rumania, forcing her to cede to the Soviet Union the province of Bessarabia, which had been taken from Russia in 1918, and also the northern Bukovina, about which nothing whatsoever had been said in the September agreement with Germany.

**Growth of Friction Between Germany and the Soviet Union.** The German-Soviet relationship had by this time been subjected to a considerable strain. The Germans had considered the Finnish war unnecessary, and their sympathies, like those of the western Allies, were wholeheartedly with the Finns. The startling haste and lack of consideration for German prestige and German interests with which the Soviet government pursued its advantage in the Baltic countries also made a bad impression in Germany. The seizure of the Bukovina was regarded as an outright imposition on German patience. As for Bessarabia, the Germans had indeed been warned, in the secret protocol to the Nonaggression Pact, of the Soviet interest in this province. They had, in their eagerness to get an agreement, unwisely expressed (in the same document) their disinterestedness in the region. But they were highly irritated by the manner in which the Soviet government proceeded to exploit these concessions.

A particular source of German resentment arose in connection with the repatriation to Germany of the large German minorities resident in these various eastern European countries. These repatriations had to be carried out by the Germans in liaison with the Soviet police officials to whose mercies the inhabitants of these regions had now been entrusted. The xenophobic hostility of these representatives of the N.K.V.D., together with their sullen unhelpfulness in the many problems of the repatriation, infuriated the many Germans who came into contact with them in this work.

**The Three-Power Pact.** The summer of 1940, marked as it was by Hitler's probings and vacillations in the question of the invasion of England, was a period of great uncertainty in European diplomacy generally. Moscow, too, took a waiting attitude. The Soviet leaders followed with rapt and anxious attention not only the evidences of the development of Hitler's plans with respect to England but also the maneuvers which were now in progress with a view to determining Japan's relationship to the European struggle.

As part of the 1939 agreement, the Germans had undertaken to exert their influence in Tokyo to cause the Japanese government to take a less hostile and menacing attitude toward the Soviet Union. Whether for this reason or because they, too, were waiting to see how the European war developed, the Japanese refrained, in the months that followed the outbreak of the European war, from pursuing the aggressive probing actions they had recently been conducting along the Soviet and Outer Mongolian borders (see p. 97-98).

The fall in July, 1940, of the relatively moderate Yonai cabinet in Tokyo, plus the tremendous opportunities presented to the Japanese by Hitler's defeat of the colonial powers of Holland and France and by England's difficulties, produced a new situation, and brought to a head the negotiations which led to the conclusion, on September 27, 1940, of the Three-Power Pact by Germany, Italy, and Japan.

The formal association of Japan with the Axis made more acute the need, already created by the many events of the preceding year, for clarification of the relationship of the Soviet Union to the two great coalitions. Ribbentrop, in particular, was anxious that the Soviet Union should cast its lot finally with the Axis by joining the new pact, thus barring the road to any Soviet maneuvering between the two warring camps. For this reason, and because of the many frictions and conflicts of interest that had now arisen along the demarcation line in eastern Europe (particularly in Finland and the Balkans), a need was felt for a new clarification of the German-Russian relationship. A visit of Molotov to Berlin was therefore arranged for November 12-14.

**The Molotov Visit.** Hitler, by this time, appears already to have been seriously contemplating an attack on the Soviet Union the following spring. England's refusal to come to terms, the failure of the air attack on England, and the obvious difficulty of an invasion of the British Isles, had presented new and unexpected problems for German policy. One of the alternatives to an invasion of England, and one strongly urged on Hitler by his advisers, was an attempt to strike England's world position on its Mediterranean flank, by a thrust through the Balkans. But here Stalin's policy, based so obviously on an ambition to bring the Balkans under Soviet control, was a thorn in the German side. Moreover, there was now bound to be at least a long delay in the final destruction of England. In this situation, two great factors of uncertainty loomed out for the German planners. One was the United States, and the growing possibility of its military association with Great Britain. The other was the Soviet Union, with its extensive armed forces and its ambivalent position toward the war. About the first, there was little that could be done, other than to encourage the Japanese to make trouble for the United States. But the second was accessible to the striking power of the great German army, now idling and in danger of losing its tone if unemployed.

Moved by these reflections, and already strongly inclined to the idea of attacking Russia, Hitler was in no mood, at the time of the Molotov visit, to go out of his way to appease Soviet interests. Molotov, on the other hand, came to Berlin with a set of demands which evidently represented a serious misapprehension on the part of the Soviet leaders as to the strength of their position. Choosing to regard a Soviet adherence to the Three-Power Pact as an important concession on their part to the Axis, for which a high price could be exacted, the Soviet leaders declined even to discuss such adherence before obtaining satisfaction with regard to certain of their aspirations in eastern Europe and elsewhere. They demanded the removal of German troops from Finland, where the Germans now enjoyed, by courtesy of the Finnish government, the right of military passage to the German-occupied northern Norway. They insisted that Bulgaria should be recognized, in effect, as a dependency of the Soviet Union. They demanded German sanction for the establishment of Soviet land and naval bases in the vicinity of the Bosporus and the Dardanelles. In addition to this, the area south of the Caspian, down to the Persian Gulf, was to be recognized as an area for Soviet expansion. Finally, Japan was to be persuaded to renounce her coal and oil concessions in Northern Sakhalin. Short of the satisfaction of these demands, Molotov would not even discuss the question of Soviet adherence to the Three-Power Pact. This position, to which Molotov clung with wooden stubbornness throughout the Berlin talks, was later reaffirmed in a note to the German government of November 25. (*See Document No. 34.*)

For Hitler, this was the end. Less than a fortnight after the receipt of this German note he secretly instructed his generals to begin preparations for the attack on Russia. On December 18, formal orders were issued for this military operation, to be known as "Operation Barbarossa," and to begin the following spring.

**The Final Phase.** From the turn of the year 1940-1941, whether Stalin realized it or not, the fate of Russia's relation to the European war was already sealed by Hitler's decision. Evading an answer to the Soviet note of November 25, the Germans at first masked their military preparations behind (a) the conclusion (January 1941) of a new Soviet-German trade agreement and (b) the sale to the Soviet Union (against monetary compensation) of the Suwalki district, on the German-Lithuanian border, for which the Russians had been pressing. But in March and April 1941, the Germans showed, in the conduct of their various military campaigns in Bulgaria, Greece, and Yugoslavia, a studied indifference to Soviet feelings and to known Soviet desiderata. Warnings of the true German intentions had by this time reached the Soviet government from various quarters (including the American Department of State). By the middle of April the Soviet leaders can scarcely have been under any illusions as to what was afoot.

**The Soviet-Japanese Neutrality Pact.** One episode remained to be experienced before the German forces began their attack. On March 23 the Japanese Foreign Minister, Yosuke Matsuoka, arrived in Moscow in the course of a diplomatic journey to Moscow, Berlin, and

Rome. His purpose, in the words of two American historians, was "to seek a political agreement with the Kremlin which would assure Japan a free hand in the western Pacific." [3] He passed through Moscow twice, and had two sets of interviews with the Soviet statesmen: one on March 23-24, on his way to western Europe; the other—in the period April 7-13, on his return trip to Tokyo. The Japanese, in despatching Matsuoka on his trip, had evidently thought that it now would be possible to talk to Moscow in terms of a far-reaching clarification of Soviet-Japanese relations, including Moscow's adherence to the Three-Power Pact, as well as a number of other concessions on the Soviet side. But Matsuoka found the Russians unwilling to meet Japanese wishes with regard to the long-standing problems of Soviet-Japanese relations (particularly the status of the island of Sakhalin). The Germans, too, though unwilling to reveal to the Japanese their plans for an early attack on Russia, managed to convey to Matsuoka that their enthusiasm for bringing Russia into the Three-Power Pact had now waned. Both Russians and Germans were anxious, however, that Japan should move southward, against the colonial possessions of the European powers in the Southeast Asia region (in the first instance, against Singapore) as soon as possible: the Germans, because they wished to see the United States and England embroiled with Japan and wished also to keep the Japanese out of Siberia during the pending war with Russia; the Russians, because they wished to see Japan embroiled with the United States and England, as a means of relieving pressure on their eastern frontier. Both Moscow and Berlin were anxious, therefore, to see a relaxation of tension between Russia and Japan. By the time of Matsuoka's second visit in Moscow, furthermore, Stalin had apparently become seriously concerned about the possibility of a German attack. He now realized the advantages of a deal with Japan, both from the standpoint of engaging Japan's attention elsewhere in the forthcoming crucial period, and as a possible means of pleasing and placating the Germans. The result was the conclusion, on the final day of

[3] William L. Langer and S. Everett Gleason, *The Undeclared War 1940-1941* (New York, 1953), p. 343.

Matsuoka's stay in Moscow (April 13), of a Japanese-Soviet Neutrality Pact. The pact provided that both parties would remain neutral in case either party were attacked by one or more third powers. Japan agreed to respect the integrity of the Mongolian People's Republic. In return, the Soviet government promised to respect the integrity of Manchukuo. The Japanese secretly agreed to settle, in a manner acceptable to Moscow, the thorny question of their concessions on the Northern Sakhalin.[4]

**The German Attack.** It was on the occasion of Matsuoka's departure from Moscow, on the evening of the day of the signing of the pact, that Stalin unexpectedly appeared at the railway station to see the Japanese statesman off, and startled everyone by the demonstrative and emotional words of friendship which he addressed to the German representatives present on the platform. Unquestionably, he was now torn between concern over the real possibility of a German attack, and suspicion that the warnings he was receiving from the western governments represented attempts to put him at odds with the Germans. This anguish must have been increased by the news of Hess' flight to England on May 10—an event which could only have been interpreted in Stalin's suspicious mind as certain proof that a secret collusion between England and Germany existed.

In the final weeks before the Germans struck, Stalin behaved very strangely. He seemed paralyzed by the danger now advancing upon him. He resolutely refused to give any outward recognition of this danger, or to discuss it with foreign representatives. He apparently declined even to place the Soviet armed forces under any special form of alert. Neither Soviet officialdom nor the Soviet people were given any forewarning of the pending catastrophe. It was, therefore, against a startled and in many respects unprepared Russia that the full might of Hitler's war machine was launched in the early hours of June 22nd, 1941.

Whether the Soviet leaders, by a different policy, could have averted this disaster must remain a matter of speculation. They must have known, in concluding the Nonaggression Pact of September 1939, that they would

[4] *Ibid.*, p. 355.

require a long spoon if they were to sup successfully with this particular dinner-partner. Hitler's nature was of course such that no particular mode of behavior on the part of his adversaries or intended victims could give any final immunity to the manifestations of his aggressiveness. It is evident, on the other hand, that the characteristic features of Stalin's diplomacy—the secretiveness, the suspiciousness, and the grasping arrogant nature of Soviet behavior in moments of real or fancied success—played a part in accelerating the change of heart that brought Hitler to the attack. This decision, it must be recalled, was taken in the light of strong contrary advice within Hitler's own entourage. The power of this advice would presumably have been greater had Stalin shown himself, vis-à-vis his German partners, more restrained in his ambitions, more moderate and considerate in his methods, more forthcoming and confident in his utterances; whether it would have been great enough remains a matter of conjecture.

Of Soviet Russia, as of the western Allies, it can only be said that any policy designed to avert the catastrophes of 1939 to 1945 would—to have had any strong prospects of success—have had to be inaugurated many years before these catastrophes actually matured.

# — 10 —

# CONCLUSIONS

The dominant motive of Soviet statesmanship, over the period under review, was the preservation of the integrity of Soviet power within Russia. In this sense, Soviet diplomacy may be said to have been successful; for this integrity was indeed preserved: Soviet power was not overthrown; it was in fact strong enough, by 1941, to stand even the terrible ordeal to which it was put by the German invasion. It is true that this would never have been the case had its opponents, foreign and domestic, not been divided at crucial moments. At other crucial moments the Soviet government found itself materially aided, whether through accident or design, by policies pursued by outside powers. Geography also helped. None of this changes the fact that Soviet diplomacy was generally conducted with extraordinary energy and resourcefulness, and often with a brutal and effective tactical realism. Without these resources of the diplomatic effort, this generally favorable result might, again, never have been achieved.

Yet one must remember that the problem with which Soviet diplomacy had to deal was in part self-created. If it were not for the peculiar personality and behavior of the Soviet regime itself—its ideological preconceptions against the West, its cruelties at home, the traditionally Russian sense of suspicion and insecurity vis-à-vis the outside world by which it was inspired, and above all its cultivation for domestic-political purposes of the myth of a hostile external environment—the problem of the protection of Soviet power within Russia might never have been what it was.

The Soviet regime was of course at all times the subject of very real hostility in some western quarters. This was manifested during the intervention of 1918-1920—although even here it was not the only motive which played a part. There was, again, nothing that was fancied, and little that was provoked, in the Hitlerite danger.

But it must be said that the Soviet leaders consistently added to the dimensions of this problem by their own actions. To justify the dictatorship without which they felt unable to maintain themselves in power at home, they never hesitated to depict the outside world as more inimical and menacing than it actually was, and to treat it accordingly. In this way they not only encumbered themselves with imagined burdens that had no real existence, but they also provoked real fears and resentments that need otherwise never have existed. It is against these various elements of recalcitrance, some real, some unreal, all of them superimposed on the normal rivalries and asperities that make international life so difficult in the best of circumstances, that Soviet diplomacy was obliged to do battle.

# Part II

# DOCUMENTS

## — Document No. 1 —

## DECREE ON PEACE, NOVEMBER 8, 1917[1]

*Drafted by Lenin himself in the fall of 1917, and approved by the II All-Russian Congress of Soviets of Workers', Soldiers', and Peasants' Deputies on the second day of the November Revolution, this Decree represented the first act of foreign policy performed by the new government. It was immediately made available to the foreign press in Petrograd and was broadcast by wireless; but it was never formally addressed or communicated to the Allied governments.*

The Workers' and Peasants' Government, created by the Revolution of October 24-25 and based upon the Soviets of Workers', Soldiers', and Peasants' Deputies, proposes to all the warring peoples and their governments that they immediately enter into negotiations for a just, democratic peace.

A just or democratic peace, such as the majority of the workers and the toiling classes of the warring countries, exhausted, tormented and ravaged by the war, are yearning for—the sort of peace which the Russian workers and peasants have demanded in the most definite and insistent way since the overthrow of the Tsarist monarchy—this sort of peace, in the opinion of this Government,

[1] *Dokumenty vneshnei politiki SSSR* (Documents of the Foreign Policy of the USSR), Vol. I (Moscow, 1957), pp. 11-14.

would be an immediate peace without annexations (i.e., without the seizure of foreign territories and without the forced incorporation of foreign peoples) and without indemnities.

Under annexation or the seizure of foreign territories the Government understands, in accordance with the sense of justice of democracy in general and of the toiling classes in particular, any incorporation into a large or powerful state of a small or weak people without the precise, clear and voluntarily expressed concurrence and desire of that people, regardless of the time at which this forced incorporation occurred, regardless of the stage of development of the people thus forcefully incorporated or held within the borders of the given state, and regardless of whether this people lives in Europe or in remote overseas countries.

If any people is held by force within the borders of a given state, if such a people in defiance of its expressed wish—whether this wish be expressed in the press, in meetings of the populace, in the decisions of a party, or in uprisings against the national yoke—is not given the right of deciding, free of every form of duress, by free elections, without the presence of the armed forces of the incorporating state or any more powerful state, what form of national existence it wishes to have—if these circumstances prevail, then the incorporation of such a state should be called annexation, i.e., an act of seizure and force.

The Government considers that it would be the greatest of crimes against humanity to continue this war only to determine how the strong and rich nations should divide among themselves the weak peoples they have seized, and it solemnly declares its determination to sign at once a peace putting an end to this war on the terms indicated, equally just for all peoples without exception.

At the same time the Government declares that it by no means considers the above-mentioned terms to be in the nature of an ultimatum; it is prepared, that is, to examine any and every other terms of peace, insisting only that they be put forward at once by someone of the warring parties, and that they be completely explicit—that every form of ambiguity and secrecy be absolutely excluded in the process of their advancement.

For its part, the Government abolishes secret diplomacy, expressing its firm intention to conduct all negotiations entirely openly before the entire people, and proceeding immediately to the publication of the secret treaties ratified or concluded from February to October 25, 1917, by the government of the landlords and the capitalists. The Government declares rescinded, immediately and unconditionally, the entire substance of these secret treaties, directed as they were for the most part to the advantage and privilege of the Russian landlords and capitalists and to the maintenance or the increase of the annexations of the Great-Russians.

In appealing to the governments and peoples of all countries to enter immediately into open negotiations for the conclusion of peace, the Government declares its own readiness to conduct such negotiations either by written communication or by telegraph or by talks between representatives of various countries or at a conference of such representatives. To facilitate such negotiations the Government is appointing its own representatives to neutral countries.

The Government proposes to all the governments and peoples of all the warring countries that they at once conclude an armistice, and holds it to be desirable that this armistice be concluded for a period of not less than three months—for a period, that is, sufficient for the completion of peace talks in which there would participate representatives of all peoples and all nationality groups, without exception, who have been involved in the war or forced to take part in it, and sufficient for the convening of assemblies of accredited people's representatives of all countries for the final ratification of the terms of peace.

In approaching the governments and peoples of all the warring countries with this proposal, the Provisional Workers' and Peasants' Government of Russia also appeals in particular to the class-conscious workers of the three leading world peoples and greatest states participating in the war: England, France and Germany. The workers of these countries have rendered the greatest service to the cause of progress and socialism. The great examples of the Chartist movement in England; the series of revolutions of universal historical significance carried out by the French proletariat; finally, the heroic struggle against the law of exclusion in Germany and the long persistent, disciplined work, exemplary for workers of all the world, performed in the creation of mass proletariat organizations in Germany—all these models of proletarian heroism and historical creativity are for us a guarantee that the workers of these countries will understand the tasks, now before them, of the liberation of humanity from the horrors of war and its consequences, and that these workers will help us, by their comprehensive, decisive and devotedly energetic activity, to carry to a successful conclusion the work of peace, and with it, the work of liberating the toiling and exploited masses of the population from every form of slavery and exploitation.

## — Document No. 2 —

# LENIN'S SPEECH, MARCH 7, 1918[2]

*The following are excerpts from the long and powerful speech which Lenin delivered on March 7, 1918, before the VII Congress of the Russian Communist Party, which was then debating the attitude to be taken in the question of ratification of the Brest-Litovsk Treaty. These excerpts will serve to illustrate not just Lenin's views on this particular subject but several outstanding features of his thinking at this time. He was pleading with his comrades, in this speech, to abandon the futile romanticism of high-sounding revolutionary "phrases" and to accept the bitter realities of their situation, which dictated ratification of the treaty.*

[2] Lenin, *Sochineniya* (Complete Works), Vol. 27 (Moscow, 1950), pp. 72-73, 76-81.

✓ ✓ ✓

. . . History has now placed us in an exceptionally difficult situation; we are obliged, while carrying out unprecedentedly difficult organizational work, to undergo a series of painful defeats. If we look at this from the world historical standpoint, there can be no doubt that the prospects for final victory of our revolution would be hopeless if it were to remain alone and if it were not for the revolutionary movement of other countries. While it is true that we took everything into the hands of the Bolshevik Party alone, we did this—we took all this upon ourselves—in the conviction that the revolution was ripening in all countries and that in the final conclusion—but not in the beginning of all things—whatever difficulties we might experience, whatever defeats fate might hold in store for us, the international socialist revolution would materialize. . . . Our salvation from all these difficulties —I repeat—is in the general European revolution. . . .

. . . The [German] revolution will not come as soon as we expected. This history has shown. We must know how to accept it as a fact, and to reckon with it, that the world socialist revolution in the advanced countries cannot begin as easily as revolution began in Russia. . . .

. . . We are just approaching the painful period of the beginning of socialist revolutions. This is a fact. We do not know, no one knows, perhaps it is quite impossible to know—whether it will triumph in the course of a few weeks or in a few days; no one can depend on it. We must be prepared for extraordinary difficulties, for infinitely painful defeats, which are inevitable because the revolution in Europe has not yet begun, though it may begin tomorrow. . . .

If we contrived [in entering the Duma in 1907] to remain revolutionaries, to work in painful circumstances and to work our way out of that situation again, we can do it now, because what we are faced with is not just our caprice, it is an objective necessity which has arisen for us in a country ruined to the last degree—has arisen because the European revolution, against our wishes, has dared to be late, and German imperialism, against our wishes, has dared to attack.

Here we must know how to retreat. . . . If you do

not know how to adapt yourself, if you are not inclined to crawl on your belly through the mud, then you are not a revolutionary but a chatterbox; and I am asking you to take this course not because it pleases me but because there is no other path, because history has not shaped itself in so pleasant a way that all revolutions ripen simultaneously. . . .

We are entering upon a period of the most onerous defeats, inflicted by an imperialism armed to the teeth on a country which has demobilized its army, which had to demobilize it. That which I predicted has come entirely true: in place of the Brest treaty we have received a peace much more humiliating, by the fault of those who did not accept it [the earlier one]. . . .

. . . When it is a question of ratifying this Tilsit peace, this unheard-of peace, more humiliating and more predatory than Brest, my answer is: absolutely yes. . . . We are now signing the peace, we have a breathing space, we will use this breathing space for the better defense of our country. . . . We will use this breathing space to persuade our people to unite and to do battle; we will use it to say to the Russian workers and peasants: "Learn self-discipline, a strict discipline, or you will lie under the heel of the German boot as you are now lying and as you must inevitably lie so long as you do not learn to fight and to create an army capable not of fleeing but of accepting unheard-of hardships." All this is inescapable, because the German revolution has not yet been born and no one can guarantee that it will come tomorrow.

## — Document No. 3 —

# SOVIET NOTE, MARCH 5, 1918[3]

*This document, handed by Trotsky, with Lenin's approval, to Raymond Robins for transmission to the American government, represents the farthest the Soviet government went in evincing interest in Allied military assistance during the Brest-Litovsk crisis. It will be noted that it was merely a query and committed the Soviet government to nothing.*

✓ ✓ ✓

In case (a) the all-Russian congress of the Soviets will refuse to ratify the peace treaty with Germany, or (b) if the German government, breaking the peace treaty, will renew the offensive in order to continue its robbers' raid, or (c) if the Soviet government will be forced by the actions of Germany to renounce the peace treaty—before or after its ratification—and to renew hostilities—

In all these cases it is very important for the military and political plans of the Soviet power for replies to be given to the following questions:

1. Can the Soviet government rely on the support of the United States of North America, Great Britain, and France in its struggle against Germany?

2. What kind of support could be furnished in the nearest future, and on what conditions—military equipment, transportation supplies, living necessities?

3. What kind of support would be furnished particularly and especially by the United States?

Should Japan—in consequence of an open or tacit understanding with Germany or without such an under-

[3] *Russian-American Relations, March, 1917-March, 1920: Documents and Papers,* Eds., C. K. Cumming and Walter W. Pettit (New York, 1920), pp. 81-82.

standing—attempt to seize Vladivostok and the Eastern-Siberian Railway, which would threaten to cut off Russia from the Pacific Ocean and would greatly impede the concentration of Soviet troops toward the East about the Urals—in such case what steps would be taken by the other allies, particularly and especially by the United States, to prevent a Japanese landing on our Far East, and to insure uninterrupted communications with Russia through the Siberian route?

In the opinion of the Government of the United States, to what extent—under the above-mentioned circumstances—would aid be assured from Great Britain through Murmansk and Archangel? What steps could the Government of Great Britain undertake in order to assure this aid and thereby to undermine the foundation of the rumors of the hostile plans against Russia on the part of Great Britain in the nearest future?

All these questions are conditioned with the self-understood assumption that the internal and foreign policies of the Soviet government will continue to be directed in accord with the principles of international socialism and that the Soviet government retains its complete independence of all non-socialist governments.

## — Document No. 4 —

# SOVIET NOTE TO BRITISH REPRESENTATIVE, APRIL 6, 1918[4]

*Upon learning of the British and Japanese landings of marines at Vladivostok on April 5, 1918, the Soviet government sent identical notes of the following tenor to the British, French, and American representatives in Moscow.*

[4] *Dokumenty vneshnei politiki SSSR,* Vol. I, *op. cit.,* pp. 230-231.

The People's Commissariat for Foreign Affairs, referring to the oral statements made to you by the Acting Deputy concerning the extremely unfavorable impression made in Russia by the landing of Japanese and English troops at Vladivostok, the actions of which are clearly directed against Soviet power, and concerning the extremely unfavorable influence which this violent intrusion of a foreign armed force into the territory of the Republic will exert on the relations between the latter and the government you represent, considers it necessary to remind you of the extremely tense situation which has been created by this measure, so strikingly hostile to the Republic and its system, and to point out once more that the only way out from the situation that has arisen is the immediate removal of the forces that have been landed —also that a definite and immediate clarification of the relationship of your Government to the fait accompli in Vladivostok is absolutely necessary.

[Signed] Acting Deputy People's Commissar
for Foreign Affairs [Chicherin]

## — Document No. 5 —

# RESOLUTION CONSTITUTING THE COMINTERN, MARCH 4, 1919[5]

[5] Jane Degras, Ed., *The Communist International 1919-1943, Documents,* Vol. I, *1919-1922* (London, 1956), p. 17. Published by Oxford University Press, on behalf of the Royal Institute of International Affairs; used by permission.

*The following is the text of the resolution setting up the Communist International. It was approved by all the participants except the German delegate. The German communists subsequently adhered.*

✓ ✓ ✓

The representatives of the Communist Party of German-Austria, of the left Social-Democratic Party of Sweden, of the Social-Democratic Revolutionary Workers' Federation of the Balkans, of the Communist Party of Hungary, move that the Communist International be founded.

1. The fight for the dictatorship of the proletariat requires a united, resolute, international organization of all communist elements which adopt this platform.

2. The foundation of the Communist International is the more imperative since now at Berne, and possibly later elsewhere also, an attempt is being made to restore the old opportunist International and to rally to it all the confused and undecided elements of the proletariat. It is therefore essential to make a sharp break between the revolutionary proletariat and the social-traitor elements.

3. If the conference now sitting at Moscow were not to found the Third International, the impression would be created that the communist parties are not at one; this would weaken our position and increase the confusion among the undecided elements of the proletariat in all countries.

4. To constitute the Third International is therefore an unconditional historical imperative which must be put into effect by the international communist conference now sitting in Moscow.

## — Document No. 6 —

# SOVIET PROPOSALS TO PEACE CONFERENCE, MARCH 19, 1919[6]

*One of the exchanges between the Allies and the Soviet government which took place during the Paris Peace Conference was conducted by Mr. William C. Bullitt, who visited Moscow in March 1919 and had private discussions with Lenin on behalf of Colonel Edward M. House and the British Prime Minister, David Lloyd George. The proposals, handed to Bullitt by Lenin (of which the following are excerpts) show the Soviet government to have been willing to go quite far, at that time, in facilitating a departure of the Allied troops from Russia. Bullitt was most unjustly disavowed by Wilson and Lloyd George, on his return, and no serious consideration was ever given by the Allies to Lenin's proposals. Bullitt was later (1933) to become the first American Ambassador to the Soviet Union.*

✓ ✓ ✓

1. All existing *de facto* Governments which have been set up on the territory of the former Russian Empire and Finland to remain in full control of the territories which they occupy at the moment when the armistice becomes effective, except insofar as the conference may agree upon the transfer of territories; until the peoples inhabiting the territories controlled by these *de facto* Governments shall themselves determine to change their Governments. The Russian Soviet Government, the other Soviet Governments, and all other Governments which have been set up on the territory of the former Russian Empire, the Allied and Associated Governments, and the other Gov-

[6] *Papers Relating to the Foreign Relations of the United States, 1919, Russia* (Washington, 1937), pp. 78-80.

ernments which are operating against the Soviet Governments, including Finland, Poland, Galicia, Roumania, Armenia, Azerbaidjan, and Afghanistan, to agree not to attempt to upset by force the existing *de facto* Governments which have been set up on the territory of the former Russian Empire and the other Governments signatory to this agreement.

The Allied and Associated Governments to undertake to see to it that the *de facto* governments of Germany do not attempt to upset by force the *de facto* governments of Russia. The *de facto* governments which have been set up on the territory of the former Russian Empire to undertake not to attempt to upset by force the *de facto* governments of Germany.

2. The economic blockade to be raised and trade relations between Soviet Russia and the Allied and Associated countries to be reestablished under conditions which will ensure that supplies from the Allied and Associated countries are made available on equal terms to all classes of the Russian people.

3. The Soviet Governments of Russia to have the right of unhindered transit on all railways and the use of all ports which belong to the former Russian Empire and to Finland and are necessary for the disembarkation and transportation of passengers and goods between their territories and the sea; . . .

4. The citizens of the Soviet Republics of Russia to have the right of free entry into the Allied and Associated countries as well as into all countries which have been formed on the territory of the former Russian Empire and Finland; also the right of sojourn and of circulation and full security, provided they do not interfere in the domestic politics of those countries. . . .

5. The Soviet Governments, the other Governments which have been set up on the territory of the former Russian Empire and Finland, to give a general amnesty to all political opponents, offenders and prisoners. . . .

All prisoners of war of non-Russian powers detained in Russia, likewise all nationals of those powers now in Russia to be given full facilities for repatriation. . . .

6. Immediately after the signing of this agreement, all troops of the Allied and Associated Governments and other non-Russian governments to be withdrawn from

Russia and military assistance to cease to be given to anti-Soviet Governments which have been set up on the territory of the former Russian Empire. . . .

The Soviet Government of Russia undertakes to accept the foregoing proposal provided it is made not later than April 10th, 1919.

## — Document No. 7 —

# LENIN'S SPEECH, NOVEMBER 21, 1920[7]

*In this passage from Lenin's speech on the internal and external tasks of the Party, delivered at the Moscow Guberniya Party Conference on November 21, 1920, he addressed himself to the emerging situation as compared with the original Bolshevik calculations of 1917-1918. Note both the polemic exaggeration and the extreme self-centeredness of the reasons he gives for the failure of the intervention. Nothing in this passage would suggest that any of the Allied powers might, in the period 1917-1920, have had* other *important preoccupations than the intervention in Russia, or reasons of their own, other than pro-Soviet sentiments within their military forces, for terminating the intervention. There also is nothing to suggest that opinions even in conservative circles in the West were sorely divided on the wisdom of intervention. It could only be assumed, from these words, that the intervention had represented a single-minded, concentrated, all-out military effort of western capitalism.*

✓ ✓ ✓

When three years ago we raised the question of the tasks and conditions of victory for the proletarian revolution in Russia, we always stated positively that this vic-

[7] Lenin, *op. cit.*, Vol. 31 (1952), pp. 383-384.

tory could not be a firm one unless it was supported by proletarian revolution in the West, that correct appreciation of our revolution was possible only from the international standpoint. In order to win a firm victory, we had to achieve the victory of the proletarian revolution in all, or at least in a number, of the main capitalist countries. Now, after three years of embittered, persistent warfare, we see in what respects our predictions were *not* justified and in what respects they *were* justified. They were not justified in the sense that no rapid and simple solution of this question [of world revolution] has been found. Of course, none of us expected that so unequal a struggle as the struggle between Russia and all the capitalist countries of the world could go on for as long as three years. But it turned out that neither one side nor the other—neither the Soviet Russian Republic nor the entire remaining capitalist world—won victory or suffered defeat, and at the same time it turned out that if our predictions were not simply and rapidly and directly fulfilled, they were fulfilled to the extent that they gave us the main thing; for the main thing was to preserve the possibility of existence for proletarian power and for the Soviet Republic, even in case of a delay of the socialist revolution throughout the world. In that respect it must be said that the international situation has now developed in such a way as to give the best, the most exact confirmation of all our calculations and of our entire policy.

## — Document No. 8 —

# SPEECH BY L. B. KAMENEV, MARCH 15, 1921[8]

[8] Xenia Joukoff Eudin and Harold H. Fisher, *Soviet Russia and the West, 1920-1927,* pp. 93-94. Copyright 1957 by the Board of Trustees of Leland Stanford Junior University; reprinted with permission of the publishers, Stanford University Press.

*In this passage, Kamenev, a Politburo member, justifies to the delegates to the X Party Congress the decision to attempt to enlist foreign capital for the reconstruction of the Russian economy. While he has in mind primarily the concessions policy, the underlying considerations outlined in his statement are relevant to relations with the capitalist world as a whole.*

. . . Comrades, during the last three years we needed an army to defend the existence of Soviet Russia. Now we can say boldly: In order to defend her existence, Soviet Russia must develop her productive forces with the greatest possible speed, and on a gigantic scale. Once we enter the arena of world economic competition, two possibilities confront us: Either by developing our productive forces we shall be victorious in this economic arena as we have been in our military efforts, or we shall be overtaken by the capitalist countries. We dare not shut our eyes to this fact. When we went to war we knew our adversary was stronger than we were, both numerically and in the superiority of his training, equipment, ammunition, tanks, guns, and planes. So now, too, we must say to ourselves: The capitalist countries are at present more powerful than we are economically; they have more engines, more machinery, more equipment, and a better organization, and they know how to manage their economy better than we do.

We must acknowledge this fact. They are stronger than we are. However, we are now in a position to prevent them from forcing us to give in to their strength. How can we do this? By developing our productive forces. This means that we must start to develop our natural resources with unheard-of rapidity.

I am now approaching a question that has worried the party: While developing our natural resources, can we save and develop our economy without the help of foreign capital? . . . Our answer is no. We can, of course, restore our economy by the heroic effort of the working masses. But we cannot develop it fast enough to prevent the capitalist countries from overtaking us, unless we call in foreign capital. We must realize this clearly; we must also explain it to the workers. . . .

. . . In developing our natural wealth, we cannot receive help from foreign capital unless we pay for it. We shall have to pay a tribute.

. . . We are paying for our economic backwardness; and, in addition, we are paying a percentage to foreign capital because the world revolution is not advancing as rapidly, not taking over control of the means of production in Western Europe as quickly, as desirable.

. . .

But we are convinced that the foreign capitalists, who will be obliged to work on the terms we offer them, will dig their own grave. Without them we cannot rearm ourselves [economically]; this is the dialectic of history; we cannot rearm ourselves [economically] without the electrification of Russia. But while strengthening Soviet Russia, developing her productive forces, foreign capital will fulfill the role Marx predicted for it when he said that capital was digging its own grave. With every additional shovel of coal, with every additional load of oil that we in Russia obtain through the help of foreign technique, capital will be digging its own grave.

Therefore, without pessimism, but with full confidence and a firm conviction that we must, at any cost, preserve the principles of socialist economy in Soviet Russia until such time as our poor and devastated country is joined by the proletarian soviet republics of other more industrially and economically advanced countries, we can resort to new measures, [the right to] which we won as the result of three years of war—i.e., to attracting the assistance of foreign capital.

. . .

## — Document No. 9 —

# MAXIM GORKY'S APPEAL FOR FAMINE RELIEF, JULY 13, 1921[9]

*Gorky was unquestionably instigated by the Party to make this appeal. By this means the Soviet leaders spared themselves the humiliation of having to appeal in their own names to the bourgeois world for aid. The appeal, it will be seen, is based squarely on cultural and humanitarian grounds. "Cultured European and American people," it is implied, should help suffering Russians—because this is the nation of Tolstoy and Dostoyevski; Soviet power, the reader is allowed to infer, is neither here nor there. Note with what care Gorky avoids identifying himself with the humanitarian sentiments to which he appeals.*

The corn [grain]-growing steppes are smitten by crop failure, caused by the drought. The calamity threatens starvation to millions of Russian people. Think of the Russian people's exhaustion by the war and revolution, which considerably reduced its resistance to disease and its physical endurance. Gloomy days have come for the country of Tolstoy, Dostoyevsky, Meneleyev [Mendeleev], Pavlov, Mussorgsky, Glinka and other world-prized men and I venture to trust that the cultured European and American people, understanding the tragedy of the Russian people, will immediately succor with bread and medicines.

If humanitarian ideas and feelings—faith in whose social import was so shaken by the damnable war and its victors' unmercifulness towards the vânquished—if faith in the creative force of these ideas and feelings, I say, must and can be restored, Russia's misfortune offers

[9] *Ibid.*, pp. 73-74.

humanitarians a splendid opportunity to demonstrate the vitality of humanitarianism. I think particularly warm sympathy in succoring the Russian people must be shown by those who, during the ignominious war, so passionately preached fratricidal hatred, thereby withering the educational efficacy of ideas evolved by mankind in the most arduous labors and so lightly killed by stupidity and cupidity. People who understand the words of agonizing pain will forgive the involuntary bitterness of my words.

I ask all honest European and American people for prompt aid to the Russian people. Give bread and medicine.

MAXIM GORKY

## — Document No. 10 —

# LENIN'S REPORT, DECEMBER 21, 1920[10]

*In his report to the Bolshevik deputies at the VIII Congress of Soviets, Lenin is here taking account of the growing interest of conservative (this is what he means by "Black Hundred"; the term is borrowed from Russian political parlance) German circles in the development of relations with Russia as an alternative to Versailles—an interest greatly stimulated by the implications of the Russian-Polish war of 1920.*

[10] Lenin, Vol. 31, *op. cit.* p. 444.

✓ ✓ ✓

. . .

Finally, let us take the relationship of England and of the entire Entente to Germany. Germany is the most advanced country, with the exception of America. . . . And here this country, bound by the Versailles Treaty, is in a situation where existence is simply impossible. In the face of this situation Germany is naturally impelled in the direction of an alliance with Russia. When Russian troops were approaching Warsaw, all of Germany was boiling. [The idea of] an alliance with Russia for this country, which is being throttled, which has the capability of unleashing gigantic productive forces—this idea has had the effect of creating in Germany a political mixture: the German Black Hundreds have gone along with the Spartacists in sympathy for the Bolsheviki. And this is entirely understandable, since it flows from economic causes—it constitutes the basis of the entire economic situation and of our foreign policy. . . .

## — Document No. 11 —

# SOVIET NOTE TO ALLIES, OCTOBER 28, 1921 [11]

*In this communication, Chicherin voiced the desire of the Soviet leaders for an international conference to establish a basis for official and economic relations between Russia and the western countries. Note, in connection with debts and claims, the proviso "for special con-*

[11] Jane Degras, Editor, *Soviet Documents on Foreign Policy*, Vol. I, *1917-1924* (London, 1951), pp. 271-272. Published by Oxford University Press on behalf of the Royal Institute of International Affairs; used by permission.

*ditions and facilities." Chicherin had in mind here that the Soviet government would consent to make payments against the old Tsarist obligations only in case it received new credits in even larger amount. Also note that while mention is made of the Tsarist debts, nothing is said of the war debt or of possible reimbursement for nationalized property.*

✓ ✓ ✓

. . . Having as its aim the interests of all the workers of Russia, the Workers' and Peasants' Government, which has emerged victorious from unparalleled ordeals of civil war and foreign intervention, offers to private enterprise and capital the opportunity of co-operating with the Workers' and Peasants' Government in the task of developing the natural wealth of Russia. The Soviet Government has re-established private trade, the private ownership of small undertakings, and the right of concession and lease with regard to large ones. It gives to foreign capital legal guarantees and a share of profit sufficient to satisfy its requirements, and to induce it to take part in the economic work of Russia. With this goal in view, the Soviet Government aims at establishing economic agreements with all the Powers for which purpose it is first of all absolutely essential that a definite peace should be concluded between Russia and the other States. In pursuit of this object the Soviet Government finds the way barred by the demand of the Powers for the recognition of the Czarist debts. The Soviet Government declares its firm conviction that no people is bound to pay the price of chains fastened upon it for centuries. But, in its unshakeable determination to arrive at an entire agreement with the other Powers, the Russian Government is inclined to make several essential and highly important concessions in regard to this question. It will thus meet the wishes of the numerous small holders of Russian bonds (especially in France), for whom the recognition of the Czarist debts is a matter of vital importance. For these reasons the Russian Government declares itself ready to recognise the obligations towards other States and their citizens which arise from State loans concluded by the Czarist Government before 1914, with the express proviso that there shall be special conditions and facilities which will enable it to carry out this undertaking. It goes without saying that a *sine qua non* for this recognition is that the Great Powers should simultaneously undertake to put an end, unreservedly and entirely, to any action which threatens either the security of the Soviet Republics and of the friendly Far Eastern Republic, or their sovereign rights or the inviolability of their frontiers; and that the Great Powers undertake to observe scrupulously the sovereignty and territorial integrity of these Republics. In other words, the Soviet Republic cannot give the undertaking in question unless the Great Powers conclude with it a definite and general peace and unless the other Powers recognise its Government. For this purpose the Russian Government proposes as a matter of urgency the calling of an international conference to deal with the above questions, to consider the claims of the Powers against Russia and of Russia against the Powers, and to draw up a definite treaty of peace between them. Only a conference of this kind can bring about a general pacification. The approaching fourth anniversary of its existence will everywhere compel recognition of the fact that the efforts of all its enemies at home and abroad have only served to consolidate the position of the Workers' and Peasants' Government as the true defender and representative of the interests of the working masses of all Russia and of the independence of that country. The further interventions planned against Soviet Russia—the existence of which is proved by numerous declarations in the leading organs of the Entente press—will only serve to strengthen the indissoluble ties which bind the working masses of Russia to the Workers' and Peasants' Government, which represents their will. But the carrying out of these plans threatens to prolong the sufferings of the working masses, and to delay the complete revival of Russia—striking, at the same time, a blow against the interests of all other nations. The proposal which the Russian Government makes is the best proof of its desire for peace with all States and for economic relations which nothing can disturb. The carrying out of this proposal harmonises with the interests of all Governments and all peoples. . . .

# — Document No. 12 —

## CHICHERIN'S OPENING SPEECH AT GENOA, APRIL 10, 1922[12]

*The Soviet Government was not pleased by the manner in which the Genoa Conference finally came about and, in agreeing to attend it, had very little hope of reaching any profitable agreements with the former Allied powers. Its purpose was primarily to split the Germans from the others and thus to prevent the formation of a united front among the main capitalist powers. Chicherin accordingly used the conference as a platform for what is called, in Soviet usage, "demonstrative diplomacy," designed to appeal to peoples behind the backs of their governments.*

✓ ✓ ✓

The Russian delegation, representing a Government which has always supported the cause of peace, welcome with particular satisfaction the declarations of the preceding speakers proclaiming the primary necessity of peace. They specially associate themselves with the declaration of the Italian Prime Minister, that here there are neither victors nor vanquished, and with that of the Prime Minister of Great Britain, assuring us that we are all here on a footing of equality.

In the first place, the Russian delegation wish to state that they have come here in the interests of peace and of the general reconstruction of the economic life of

[12] *Ibid.*, pp. 298-301.

Europe, ruined by prolonged war and by the post-war policy.

Whilst maintaining the standpoint of their communist principles, the Russian delegation recognize that in the present period of history, which permits the parallel existence of the old social order and of the new order now being born, economic collaboration between the States representing these two systems of property is imperatively necessary for the general economic reconstruction.

The Russian Government therefore attributes great importance to the first point of the Cannes resolution dealing with reciprocal recognition of different systems of property and different political and economic forms existing at the present time in different countries. The Russian delegation have come here not with the intention of engaging in propaganda for their own theoretical opinions, but in order to enter into business relations with the Governments and industrial and commercial circles of all countries on the basis of reciprocity, equality, and full and unconditional recognition. The problem of universal economic reconstruction is, in present conditions, so immense and comprehensive that it can only be solved if all countries, both European and non-European, sincerely desire to co-ordinate their efforts, and are prepared if necessary to make temporary sacrifices. The economic reconstruction of Russia, the largest State in Europe, with its incalculable natural resources, is an indispensable condition of universal economic reconstruction. Russia, on its side, declares itself fully prepared to contribute to the solution of the tasks confronting the conference by all the means at its disposal, and these means are not negligible. To meet the needs of world economy, and of the development of its productive forces, the Russian Government is ready to open its frontier, deliberately and voluntarily, for international transit trade; to grant for cultivation millions of acres of most fertile land; to grant rich timber, coal, and mining concessions, particularly in Siberia, and a number of other concessions throughout the territory of the RSFSR. It aims at economic collaboration between the industry of the West and the agriculture and industry of Russia and Siberia, of such a nature as to enlarge the basis of European industry, in regard to raw materials, grain, and fuel, to a degree far surpassing the pre-war level. A more detailed draft of a plan of general economic reconstruction can, if necessary, be presented by the Russian delegation in the course of the conference. That its realization from the financial and economic point of view is perfectly possible is clear from the fact that the capital which would have to be invested annually for this purpose, which would guarantee the future of European production, would be equal to only a small part of the annual expenditure of the countries of Europe and of America on their armies and navies. . . .

## — Document No. 13 —

# TREATY OF RAPALLO, APRIL 16, 1922[13]

*This is the text of the German-Russian agreement, concluded during the Genoa Conference, which so shook world opinion and became, in western historical memory, the symbol of German-Soviet conspiracy against Europe. As the text shows, it was in no sense an alliance.*

✓ ✓ ✓

The German Government, represented by Reichsminister Dr. Walther Rathenau, and the Government of R.S.F.S.R., represented by People's Commissar Chicherin, have agreed upon the following provisions:

[13] Leonard Shapiro, *Soviet Treaty Series,* Vol. I, *1917-1928* (Washington, D. C., 1950), pp. 168-169. Used by permission of the Georgetown University Press.

I. The two Governments agree that all questions resulting from the state of war between Germany and Russia shall be settled in the following manner:

(a) Both Governments mutually renounce repayment for their war expenses and for damages arising out of the war, that is to say, damages caused to them and their nationals in the zone of war operations by military measures, including all requisitions effected in a hostile country. They renounce in the same way repayment for civil damages inflicted on civilians, that is to say, damages caused to the nationals of the two countries by exceptional war legislation or by violent measures taken by any authority of the state of either side.

(b) All legal relations concerning questions of public or private law resulting from the state of war, including the question of the treatment of merchant ships which fell into the hands of the one side or the other during the war, shall be settled on the basis of reciprocity.

(c) Germany and Russia mutually renounce repayment of expenses incurred for prisoners of war. The German Government also renounces repayment of expenses for soldiers of the Red Army interned in Germany. The Russian Government, for its part, renounces repayment of the sums Germany has derived from the sale of Russian Army material brought into Germany by these interned troops.

II. Germany renounces all claims resulting from the enforcement of the laws and measures of the Soviet Republic as it has affected German nationals or their private rights or the rights of the German state itself, as well as claims resulting from measures taken by the Soviet Republic or its authorities in any other way against subjects of the German state or their private rights, provided that the Soviet Republic shall not satisfy similar claims made by any third state.

III. Consular and diplomatic relations between Germany and the Federal Soviet Republic shall be resumed immediately. The admission of consuls to both countries shall be arranged by special agreement.

IV. Both Governments agree, further, that the rights of the nationals of either of the two Parties on the other's territory as well as the regulation of commercial relations shall be based on the most favored nation principle. This principle does not include rights and facilities granted by the Soviet Government to another Soviet state or to any state that formerly formed part of the Russian Empire.

V. The two Governments undertake to give each other mutual assistance for the alleviation of their economic difficulties in the most benevolent spirit. In the event of a general settlement of this question on an international basis, they undertake to have a preliminary exchange of views. The German Government declares itself ready to facilitate, as far as possible, the conclusion and the execution of economic contracts between private enterprises in the two countries.

VI. Article I, Paragraph (b), and Article IV of this Agreement will come into force after the ratification of this document. The other Articles will come into force immediately.

## — Document No. 14 —

# SOVIET COMMENT ON THE RAPALLO PACT[14]

*This passage from the official Soviet History of Diplomacy, published in 1945, reflects the judgment of the Rapallo pact in retrospect by official Soviet historians, writing more than two decades later, during Russia's war with Germany of 1941-1945. Note the claim that Germany was successfully played off against the others to Russia's advantage. That the "ring of economic blockade around Soviet Russia" was broken by Rapallo is a bit of inaccurate boasting. The Allied blockade of Russia had been removed by the Supreme Allied Council two years earlier. Rapallo itself changed little in the conditions sur-*

[14] V. P. Potemkin, Editor, *Istoriya diplomatii* (History of Diplomacy), Vol. III (Moscow, 1945), p. 181.

*rounding Soviet trade with western countries. What was broken at Rapallo was Russia's* political *isolation.*

⁂

The Treaty of Rapallo disrupted the effort of the Entente to create a united capitalist front against Soviet Russia. The plans for the reconstruction of Europe at the expense of the conquered countries and of Soviet Russia collapsed. Soviet diplomacy won a victory because it followed the direct instructions of Lenin. "One must know how to exploit the contradictions and conflicts among the imperialists," he said. "If we had not observed this rule we would, to the pleasure of the capitalists, have long since hung from different trees."

The diplomacy of the Entente, hoping to force Soviet Russia to its knees, and having removed the problem of reparations from the agenda of discussion as a question already settled, suffered a complete defeat. To both of the participants, on the other hand, the Rapallo Treaty brought serious political advantages. The Treaty put an end to the controversial questions of the past. In place of the Brest-Litovsk Treaty, based on force, it created new mutual relations which assured to both governments full equality and the possibility of peaceful economic collaboration. The political significance of the Rapallo Treaty was determined by three of its basic features. There was, first, the mutual cancellation of all claims; secondly, there was the reestablishment of diplomatic relations between Germany and Russia (after the border states and the eastern states, Germany was the first western European power to enter into normal diplomatic relations with Soviet Russia); thirdly and finally, there was the economic rapprochement between Russia and Germany, both of whom emerged from their isolation thanks to the Rapallo Treaty. Thus the ring of economic blockade around Soviet Russia was broken. On the other hand, Germany, too, gained the possibility of widening her trade.

# — Document No. 15 —

## COMINTERN STATEMENT, MAY 19, 1922[15]

*This statement on the Genoa Conference, drawn up in Moscow by the Executive Committee of the Communist International just as the Genoa Conference came to a close, is included in order to illustrate the way in which the world-revolutionary activities of the Comintern, for which the leaders of the Russian Communist Party were entirely responsible, went hand in hand with the efforts to develop political and commercial relations with the very capitalist governments the Comintern was endeavoring to overthrow. This document shows clearly how fiery was still the underlying hatred towards the bourgeois world, and how disingenuous were the claims at Genoa to wish to live in "peace" with it. It also confirms the extent to which the Soviet proposals at Genoa were designed for propaganda purposes.*

✓ ✓ ✓

The Genoa conference has come to an end. In the intention of its initiators it was to do nothing more nor less than restore the European economic equilibrium which was shattered by the imperialist world war. The braggarts! Nobody can get outside his own skin. The imperialist bourgeoisie cannot save Europe from economic ruin—the Europe which they made into a shambles and which for four years was laid waste and devastated.

At Genoa the bourgeoisie revealed their utter powerlessness, their complete impotence. There was a great deal of noise and the prime ministers of the richest bourgeois States attended. . . . And what was the upshot? The talk went on for several weeks. The diplo-

[15] Degras, *The Communist International,* Vol. I, *op. cit.,* pp. 344-349.

mats beat about the bush and did not stir from the spot and finally they reached a happy ending, moving with God's help from Genoa to The Hague. The petty skirmishes and quarrels of the victor States among themselves have shown the entire world how deep are the contradictions between England and France, between Japan and the United States, between Italy and France, and between the victor States and Germany. The League of Nations is a stinking corpse which the Genoa conference was unable to clear out of the way. The Entente itself is creaking at every seam, junk fit only for the lumber room. The more solemnly Lloyd George and Barthou declared their conviction that the Entente was in good health, that love and harmony reigned between England and France, the more obvious became the outworn hypocrisy and the more clearly can it be seen by every proletarian that the notorious Entente has come to the end of its resources.

Never has the decadence of bourgeois society been exposed so clearly as now. The decay and disintegration of the bourgeois State are proceeding at a gigantic pace. The outward glitter of bourgeois governments is like the hectic flush on the cheeks of a consumptive. A declining class! This is the judgment that will be made by every attentive observer who has followed the course of events at the Genoa conference. The star of the bourgeoisie has set. That is the chief lesson of Genoa.

But the working class is moving up. Its star is rising. The strength of the proletariat will grow irresistibly, slowly at first but then more quickly. The proletariat will succeed the bourgeoisie in power throughout the world. That was proved most clearly by the part played by the Russian delegation at Genoa.

. . . It was only the Soviet delegation which had a consistent programme, a comprehensive outlook, a great historical perspective which served the interests not only of proletarian Russia but all the proletariat of the entire world. Alone in Genoa the Soviet delegation represented the future of humanity while all the bourgeois delegations represented the decaying past.

The first proposal made by the Soviet delegation was for disarmament. . . . This proposal was rejected by the English and all the other imperialists.

What conclusions are the workers of the world to draw from this? The conclusion can only be that disarmament is impossible so long as the bourgeoisie remain at the helm. Disarmament is impossible without the victory of the proletarian revolution.

. . .

When the attempt was made in Genoa to despoil Soviet Russia, the first proletarian republic, the bourgeoisie formed a 'united front.' Restitution—that was the battle-cry of the bourgeoisie at Genoa. Restitution for ever! Restitution, the last cry of civilization, no salvation without restitution! . . .

Soviet Russia concluded a treaty with the bourgeois German republic. The 'democrats' and 'social-democrats' who are at the helm in Germany resisted for a long time the alliance with Soviet Russia although the entire German working class for two years unanimously demanded this alliance. Only the merciless greed which characterized the attitude of the victor States at Genoa to defeated Germany induced the present German Government to sign a treaty with Soviet Russia. The treaty between Russia and Germany signed at Rapallo is of enormous historical importance. Russia with its one hundred and fifty million population and its predominantly agrarian character, in alliance with Germany with its first-class industry, represents such powerful economic co-operation that it will break through all obstacles. On the German side the treaty was signed by the present bourgeois-menshevik government, but everybody understands that while the position of the bourgeois-menshevik German government is a temporary thing, the German working class remains. The German working class will one day inevitably conquer power in their own country. Germany will become a Soviet republic. And then, when the German-Russian treaty brings together two great Soviet republics, it will provide such unshakeable foundations for real communist construction that the old and outworn Europe will not be able to withstand it for even a few years. In this sense the fate of humanity in the next few years will be determined by the successes of the German working class. The victory of the German proletariat over 'its' bourgeoisie will involve unprecedented changes in the social structure of the whole of Europe.

When the German proletariat destroys in its country the influence of the Second and Two-and-a-half Internationals a new chapter will open in the history of mankind.

. . .

At the end of the Genoa conference the Entente representatives again made an insolent attempt to bring up the question of 'pernicious communist propaganda.' The ECCI declares that the international community of worker communists organized in the Comintern will not let its freedom be hampered by any obligations whatever. We are the deadly enemies of bourgeois society. Every honest communist will fight against bourgeois society to his last breath, in word and in deed and if necessary with arms in hand. Yes, the propaganda of the Communist International will be pernicious for you, the imperialists. It is the historical mission of the Communist International to be the grave-digger of bourgeois society. No offence meant. So long as by your very existence you insult the feelings of every class-conscious worker, so long as your foul breath infects the entire world, so long as a handful of millionaires continue to build their welfare on the bones of the working class, in short so long as your capitalist social system continues to exist, the 'pernicious' propaganda of the communists will not cease. . . .

Workers of France, it is now up to you. Do everything in your power to overthrow Barthou's Government which brings shame on the workers of France. Settle accounts with the reactionary gangs who are destroying France and want to plunder Soviet Russia.

Workers of England, you have been fighting for years for the recognition of Soviet Russia and for years your bourgeoisie, helped by the social traitors, Henderson, MacDonald, and co. have been throwing sand in your eyes. Has not the Genoa conference opened your eyes?

Workers of Japan, even the predatory European Governments found themselves obliged to sign the treaty in which they undertook not to attack Soviet Russia. Only the representatives of your bloodthirsty Government demanded that an exception be made in its case. They want to continue with their daily raids on the working masses of the Far Eastern Republic. Japan is now in a prerevolutionary period. A significant part even of the Japanese bourgeoisie is opposed to the present regime. Place yourselves at the head of the ripening revolution. Seize the Japanese monarchy by the throat and place your foot on its neck.

Workers of Germany, you must seize power in your country as quickly as possible. In doing so you will remove the weight on the spirit of the world proletariat and accelerate historical progress. The fate of the proletarian revolution is in your hands. Your slogan is, 'Down with the treacherous social-democrats. Down with the power of capital. Long live the workers' government.'

Workers and Red soldiers of Russia, if you still needed proof that only the Soviet Government defends the interests of the proletariat of all countries you received it in incontestable fashion at Genoa. You are living through a difficult time but the worst is already over. Guard the Soviet Government as the apple of your eye. You stand at the outposts of the proletarian world revolution. The proletarian armies of other countries will come to your help. Victory is no longer distant. . . .

## — Document No. 16 —

# STALIN'S LECTURES, APRIL 1924 [16]

*In a series of academic lectures at Sverdlovsk University, prepared immediately after Lenin's death, Stalin set forth his concept of Lenin's teachings. The following excerpts will illustrate some of the observations made about his character in the text, particularly his caution and the emphasis he placed on divisive tactics.*

[16] Eudin and Fisher, *op. cit.,* pp. 287-289.

✓ ✓ ✓

The reserves of the revolution can be:

*Direct:* (*a*) the peasantry and in general the intermediate strata of the population within the country; (*b*) the proletariat of the neighboring countries; (*c*) the revolutionary movement in the colonies and dependent countries; (*d*) the gains and achievements of the dictatorship of the proletariat—part of which the proletariat may give up temporarily, while retaining superiority of forces, in order to buy off a powerful enemy and gain a respite; and

*Indirect:* (*a*) the contradictions and conflicts among the nonproletarian classes within the country, which can be utilized by the proletariat to weaken the enemy and to strengthen its own reserves; (*b*) contradictions, conflicts, and wars (the imperialist war, for instance) among the bourgeois states hostile to the proletarian state, which can be utilized by the proletariat in its offensive or in maneuvering in the event of a forced retreat.

There is no need to speak at length about the reserves of the first category; their significance is understood by everyone. As for the reserves of the second category, whose significance is not always clear, it must be said that sometimes they are of prime importance for the progress of the revolution. . . . It must be presumed that now, when the contradictions among the imperialist groups are becoming more and more profound, and when a new war among them is becoming inevitable, reserves of this description will assume ever greater importance for the proletariat.

The task of strategic leadership is to make proper use of all these reserves to achieve the main object of the revolution at the given stage of its development.

What does making proper use of reserves mean?

It means fulfilling certain necessary conditions, of which the following must be regarded as the principal ones:

*First:* The concentration of the main forces of the revolution at the enemy's most vulnerable spot at the decisive moment when the revolution has already become ripe, when the offensive is going full speed ahead, when insurrection is knocking at the door, and when bringing the reserves up to the vanguard is the decisive condition of success. . . .

*Second:* The selection of the moment for the decisive blow, the moment for starting the insurrection, so timed [as to coincide with the moment] when the crisis has reached the climax, when it is fully apparent that the vanguard is prepared to fight to the end, the reserves are prepared to support the vanguard, the maximum consternation reins in the ranks of the enemy.

. . .

*Third:* Undeviating pursuit of the course adopted, no matter what difficulties and complications are encountered on the road toward the goal . . .

*Fourth:* Maneuvering the reserves with a view to effecting a proper retreat when the enemy is strong, when retreat is inevitable, when it is obviously disadvantageous to accept battle forced upon us by the enemy, when, with the given alignment of forces, retreat becomes the only way to ward off a blow against the vanguard and to keep the reserves intact. . . .

The purpose of this strategy is to gain time, to demoralize the enemy, and to accumulate forces in order later to assume the offensive.

The signing of the Brest-Litovsk peace may be taken as a model of this strategy, for it enabled the party to gain time, to take advantage of the conflicts in the camp of the imperialists, to demoralize the forces of the enemy, to retain the support of the peasantry, and to accumulate forces in preparation for the offensive against Kolchak and Denkin. . . .

Such are the principal conditions of correct strategic leadership. . . .

# — Document No. 17 —

# THESES ADOPTED BY II COMINTERN CONGRESS, JULY 27, 1920[17]

*These theses on the national and colonial question, drafted by Lenin, give a clear and authoritative picture of the political principles by which the Soviet government was guided in its approach to China in the 1920's. Their particular relevance to the delicate problems Stalin faced in attempting to coordinate support for the Chinese Communists with support for the Kuomintang, as described in Chapter 6, is readily apparent.*

5. The world political situation has now placed the proletarian dictatorship on the order of the day, and all events in world politics are necessarily concentrated on one central point, the struggle of the world bourgeoisie against the Russian Soviet Republic, which is rallying round itself both the soviet movements among the advanced workers in all countries, and all the national liberation movements in the colonies and among oppressed peoples, convinced by bitter experience that there is no salvation for them except in union with the revolutionary proletariat and in the victory of the Soviet power over world imperialism.

6. At the present time, therefore, we should not restrict ourselves to a mere recognition or declaration of the need to bring the working people of various countries closer together; our policy must be to bring into being

[17] Degras, *The Communist International,* Vol. I, *op. cit.,* pp. 141, 143-144.

a close alliance of all national and colonial liberation movements with Soviet Russia; the forms taken by this alliance will be determined by the stage of development reached by the communist movement among the proletariat of each country or by the revolutionary liberation movement in the undeveloped countries and among the backward nationalities.

. . .

11. In regard to the more backward States and nations, primarily feudal or patriarchal or patriarchal-peasant in character, the following considerations must be kept specially in mind:

*a.* All communist parties must support by action the revolutionary liberation movements in these countries. The form which this support shall take should be discussed with the communist party of the country in question, if there is one. This obligation refers in the first place to the active support of the workers in that country on which the backward nation is financially, or as a colony, dependent.

. . .

*d.* It is particularly important to support the peasant movement in the backward countries against the landlords and all forms and survivals of feudalism. Above all, efforts must be made to give the peasant movement as revolutionary a character as possible, organizing the peasants and all the exploited wherever possible in soviets, and thus establish as close a tie as possible between the west European communist proletariat and the revolutionary peasant movement in the East, in the colonies and backward countries.

*e.* A resolute struggle must be waged against the attempt to clothe the revolutionary liberation movements in the backward countries which are not genuinely communist in communist colours. The Communist International has the duty of supporting the revolutionary movement in the colonies and backward countries only with the object of rallying the constituent elements of the future proletarian parties—which will be truly communist and not only in name—in all the backward countries and educating them to a consciousness of their special task, namely, that of fighting against the bourgeois-democratic trend in their own nation. The Communist International should collaborate provisionally with the revolutionary movement of the colonies and backward countries, and even form an alliance with it, but it must not amalgamate with it; it must unconditionally maintain the independence of the proletarian movement, even if it is only in an embryonic stage. . . .

## — Document No. 18 —

# SOVIET APPEAL TO CHINESE PEOPLE AND GOVERNMENTS, JULY 24, 1919[18]

*This document gives a good idea of the initial approach of the Soviet leaders, on the overt governmental rather than the Comintern level, to the problem of relations with China. It was drafted in Moscow before the collapse of Kolchak and at a moment when the Soviet government was hard pressed in the civil war. It represents, therefore, a more generous pattern of Soviet intentions toward China than was apparent after Kolchak's defeat. The passage in brackets is the celebrated offer to give up the Chinese-Eastern Railway which caused considerable excitement in China and some difficulty for Soviet diplomacy in future years. Evidently the Soviet leaders had second thoughts about this proposal almost immediately after*

[18] *Dokumenty vneshnei politiki SSSR, op. cit.,* Vol. II (Moscow, 1958), pp. 221-222, with the exception of the passage in brackets. The original source of this bracketed passage is *China Year Book 1924,* p. 868. I have availed myself here, however, of the translation of this passage which is to be found in Degras, *Soviet Documents . . . ,* Vol. I, *op. cit.,* pp. 159-160.

*the document was drafted; for when it was published in the official* Izvestiya *one month later (August 26, 1919) this bracketed clause was omitted, and the Soviet government has subsequently denied that it was ever included. There appears, however, to be no doubt that this clause was present both in an official Soviet pamphlet which appeared at the time and in a telegram received by the Chinese government from a Soviet representative at Irkutsk.*

On the day when Soviet troops, having smashed the army of the counterrevolutionary despot Kolchak who has been supported by foreign bayonets and foreign gold, have victoriously entered Siberia and are moving to a union with the revolutionary peoples of Siberia, the Soviet of People's Commissars appeals in the following fraternal words to all the peoples of China:

Soviet Russia and the Soviet Red Army, after two years of war, after incredible efforts, are marching to the East across the Urals, not for purposes of coercion, not in order to enslave peoples, not for conquest. Every Siberian peasant and every Siberian worker already knows this. We are bringing to the peoples liberation from the yoke of the foreign bayonet, from the yoke of foreign gold, which are now throttling the enslaved peoples of the east, and in the first instance the Chinese people. We are bringing aid not only to the toiling classes but to the Chinese people as well, and we are taking occasion to remind this people once more of what we have been saying to it ever since the Great October Revolution of 1917 but what, perhaps, has been concealed from it by the venal American-European-Japanese press.

As soon as the Workers' Peasants' Government took power into its hands in October 1917 it addressed itself to the peoples of the world, in the name of the Russian people, with the proposal to conclude a firm and enduring peace. The foundation of this peace was to have been the renunciation of all seizures of foreign territory, the renunciation of every sort of forced annexation of foreign nationalities, and of every sort of indemnity. Every people, large or small, regardless of where situated, whether up to this time independent or included against its own will in the composition of another state, should be free in its internal life, and no authority should hold it by force within its borders.

The Workers' Peasants' Government subsequently declared void all the secret treaties concluded with Japan, China, and the former Allies, treaties by means of which the Tsar's Government, together with its Allies, enslaved the peoples of the East and above all the Chinese people, for the profit of Russian capitalists, Russian landowners, and Russian generals. The Soviet government at that time proposed to the Chinese government negotiations concerning the annulling of the Treaty of 1896, the Peking Protocol of 1901 and of all agreements with Japan from 1907 to 1916, i.e., the return to the Chinese people of everything of which it had been deprived by the Tsarist Government independently or together with the Japanese and the Allies. The negotiations in this question continued up to March 1918. Suddenly the Allies seized the Peking Government by the throat, showered the Peking mandarins and the Peking press with gold, and forced the Chinese Government to forego every sort of relations with the Russian Workers' Peasants' Government. Without awaiting the return to the Chinese people of the Manchurian Railway, Japan and the Allies seized it, broke into Siberia themselves, and even forced Chinese troops to help them in this criminal and unprecedented act of brutality. But the Chinese people and the Chinese workers and peasants were not even permitted to know the true reason for this incursion of the American, European, and Japanese beasts of prey into Manchuria and Siberia.

We are now again addressing ourselves to the Chinese people in order to open their eyes.

The Soviet Government has surrendered the conquests made by the Tsarist Government in taking Manchuria and other regions away from China. Let the peoples who inhabit these regions themselves decide in the borders of which state they wish to be included and what sort of administration they would like to set up for themselves at home.

[The Soviet Government returns to the Chinese people, without any compensation, the Chinese Eastern Railway, and all the mining, timber, gold, and other concessions seized by Russian generals, merchants, and capitalists under the Tsarist Government, under the Kerensky government, and under the brigands, Horvath, Semenov, Kolchak.]

The Soviet Government renounces the indemnities to be received from China for the Boxer uprising of 1900, and this is the third time that it is forced to say this, because, according to information we have received, despite our renunciation, this indemnity is still being collected by the Allies for the satisfaction of the whims of the former Tsarist Minister in Peking and the former Tsarist consuls in China. All these Tsarist slaves have long since been deprived of their authority, but they continue to remain in their places and, with the support of Japan and the Allies, to deceive the Chinese people. The Chinese people should know about this and should drive them from their territory as defrauders and scoundrels.

The Soviet Government renounces all special privileges and all concessions of Russian merchants on Chinese territory. Not one Russian official, priest, or missionary shall dare to interfere in Chinese affairs, and if any one of them commits a crime he shall be brought to justice by a local court. There shall be no other power, no other court, in China than the power and the courts of the Chinese people. In addition to these main points, the Soviet Government is prepared to regulate by agreement with the Chinese people, in the person of its plenipotentiary representatives, all other questions, and to liquidate once and for all the various acts of violence and injustice committed with relation to China by former Russian governments together with Japan and the Allies.

The Soviet Government knows very well that the Allies and Japan will do everything possible in order to prevent once more the voice of the Russian workers and peasants from reaching the Chinese people. The Soviet Government knows that before there can be returned to the Chinese people all that which was taken away from it, it will be necessary first to finish off the beasts of prey who have established themselves in Manchuria and Siberia. For this reason, it is now sending its message to the Chinese people, together with its Red Army, which is moving across the Urals to the East to aid the Siberian peasants and workers in order to liberate them from the bandit Kolchak and his ally the Japanese.

If the Chinese people wish to become free like the Russian people, and to avoid the fate which the Allies have been preparing for it at Versailles with a view to turning it into a second Korea or a second India, let it understand that its only ally and brother in the struggle for freedom is the Russian worker and peasant and his Red Army.

The Soviet Government proposes to the Chinese people, in the person of its government, to enter at once into official relations with us and to send its representatives to meet our army.

Deputy People's Commissar for Foreign Affairs,
L. Karakhan

## — Document No. 19 —

# STATEMENT BY STALIN, JANUARY 19, 1925[19]

I

*These observations on the dangers of intervention or a united capitalist front against the U.S.S.R. were made in the course of a speech supporting increases in the military budget. It is interesting to note that here Stalin portrayed the danger of war as a result of the national liberation movement in the colonial countries. This did not prevent him, as a skilled dialectician, from treating the national liberation movement at other times as a protection against the danger of war.*

[19] I. V. Stalin, *Sochineniya* (Complete Works), Vol. 7, *1925* (Moscow, 1952), p. 12.

✓ ✓ ✓

. . . The international situation has begun recently to undergo a fundamental change. New factors are ripening which bode for us new complications, for which we must be ready. The question of intervention again becomes an acute question of the moment.

What are the facts?

First, the strengthening of the anti-colonial and in general of the liberation movement in the East. India, China, Egypt, the Sudan—these are important bases for imperialism. Here the anti-colonial movement is growing and will continue to grow. This cannot fail to cause the commanding echelons of the great powers to be influenced against us, against the Soviets, for they know that the seeds which are falling on this fertile soil in the East are ripening and will sprout. They will definitely sprout. . . .

## — Document No. 20 —

# STALIN'S SPEECH, MAY 9, 1925[20]

*On May 9, 1925 Stalin addressed the activists of the Moscow Party Organization regarding the results of the work of the XIV Conference of the Russian Communist Party (Bolsheviki), and commented on the international situation.*

✓ ✓ ✓

. . . The stabilization of capitalism can have the effect that the imperialist groups of the advanced countries will endeavor to agree on the formation of a united front against the Soviet Union. Suppose that they are successful

[20] *Ibid.*, pp. 100-101.

in cooking up such a scheme. Suppose that they are successful in establishing something in the nature of a united front, . . . Are there grounds for believing that such an agreement against our country, or a stabilization in this field, could be in any way enduring, in any way successful? I think there are no such grounds. Why? Because, in the first place, the threat of a united front and of a joint advance of capitalists against us would create the most tremendous solidarity, drawing the entire country around the Soviet government as never before and turning it into an unassailable fortress even in greater degree than was the case, for example, at the time of the attack of the "fourteen governments." . . . You know that merely the utterance of this threat was enough to unite the entire country around the Soviet regime and against the imperialist beasts of prey. And secondly, because an attack against the Soviet country would inevitably untie a series of revolutionary knots in the rear of the adversary, disintegrating and demoralizing the ranks of the imperialists. . . . Thirdly, because our country is not alone—it has allies in the workers of the West and in the oppressed peoples of the East. It can scarcely be doubted that a war against the Soviet Union would mean a war of imperialism against its own workers and colonies. I don't have to prove that if our country is attacked we will not sit with folded hands; we will take all measures to release the lion of revolution in all the countries of the world. The leaders of the capitalist countries must be aware that we have a certain amount of experience along these lines. . . .

# — Document No. 21 —

## STALIN'S STATEMENTS, MAY 1925 [21]

*The following excerpts from statements made by Stalin in May 1925 illustrate his views on the principles by which Moscow's policy toward China should be based and on the role to be assigned to the Chinese Communists in the implementation of Moscow's policies.*

I

*In his speech on May 9, 1925 to the Moscow Communist Party organization, Stalin had this to say about the current tasks of the communist "elements" in colonial and dependent countries.*[21]

✓ ✓ ✓

Here is what is new in this field: (a) in view of the intensified export of capital from the advanced countries into the backward ones, stimulated by the stabilization of capitalism, capitalism in the colonial countries is developing and will continue to develop at a rapid pace, disrupting the old social-political conditions and creating new ones; (b) the proletariat in these countries is growing and will continue to grow at an intensified pace; (c) the revolutionary workers' movement and the revolutionary crisis in the colonies are growing and will continue to grow; (d) in this connection, certain strata of the indigenous bourgeoisie are developing and will continue to develop—the most wealthy and powerful ones—who, fearing revolution in their own countries more than they fear imperialism, prefer a dicker with imperialism to the

[21] *Ibid.*, pp. 106-108.

liberation of their own countries from imperialism, betraying in this way their own motherlands (India, Egypt, etc.); (e) in view of all this, the liberation of these countries from imperialism can be effected only in the course of a struggle against the collaborationist indigenous bourgeoisie. . . .

Hence, the task of communist elements in the colonial countries: to get together with the revolutionary elements of the bourgeoisie and above all with the peasantry against the bloc of imperialism and of the collaborationist elements of "their own" bourgeoisie, in order to conduct, at the head of the proletariat, a real revolutionary struggle for liberation from imperialism. . . .

## II

*In a speech of May 18, 1925, on the subject of the political tasks of the "University of the People's of the East," an institution functioning in Moscow for the training of Asian communist agents, Stalin had the following to say, evidently with the Kuomintang in mind.*[22] *It is curious to note that the dangers he warns against here are precisely the ones which did indeed befall the Chinese Communists, acting under Moscow's instructions, two years later, thus demonstrating that if Stalin's principles were sound, then his tactics were faulty.*

✓ ✓ ✓

. . .

In countries such as Egypt and China, where the indigenous bourgeoisie has already divided into revolutionary and collaborationist parties, but where the collaborationist portion of the bourgeoisie has not yet succeeded in fusing with imperialism, the communists can no longer take as their purpose the establishment of a united national front against imperialism. Communists in these countries should shift from the policy of the united national front to the policy of the revolutionary bloc of workers and petty bourgeoisie. In such countries this bloc may take the form of a single party, a workers'-peasants' party—provided, however, that this peculiar sort of party actually represents a bloc of those forces—

[22] *Ibid.*, pp. 146-147.

the communist party and the party of the revolutionary petty bourgeoisie. The tasks of this bloc are to expose the schizophrenia and the inconsistency of the indigenous bourgeoisie and to conduct a determined struggle with imperialism. Such a dual party is necessary and efficacious, if it does not bind the communist party hand and foot, if it does not hamper the freedom of agitational and propaganda work of the communist party, if it does not make it difficult to unite the proletariat around the communist party, if it facilitates the effective leadership of the revolutionary movement by the communist party. Such a dual party is not necessary and is not efficacious, if it does not meet these requirements, for then it can lead only to the diffusion of the communist elements among the ranks of the bourgeoisie, to the loss by the communist party of the proletarian army. . . .

## — Document No. 22 —

# SOVIET REPLY TO SECRETARY STIMSON, DECEMBER 3, 1929[23]

*This excerpt from Litvinov's reply to the representation made by the United States government in the Soviet-Chinese dispute shows how keenly Moscow resented this interference and how ably Litvinov exploited both the circumstances of the absence of diplomatic relations between the two countries and the fact that the Chinese-Soviet dispute was well on its way to being composed, under Soviet military pressure, at the moment when Secretary Stimson intervened.*

[23] Degras, *Soviet Documents on Foreign Policy, op. cit.*, Vol. II, *1925-1932* (London, 1952), pp. 407-408. Published by Oxford University Press on behalf of the Royal Institute of International Affairs; used by permission.

✓ ✓ ✓

6. The Soviet Government notes that the Government of the United States has addressed its note to the Soviet Government at the moment when the Soviet and Mukden Governments have already agreed upon a number of conditions and are conducting direct negotiations which may make possible the speedy settlement of the Soviet-Chinese conflict. In view of this circumstance the aforementioned note cannot but be regarded as totally unjustifiable pressure on the negotiations, and consequently cannot in any way be considered as a friendly act.

7. The Soviet Government further observes that the treaty of Paris on the renunciation of war does not make provision for the delegation of the function of guardian of the pact to any State or group of States. In any case the Soviet Government has never announced its agreement that any Governments should, of their own accord or in consultation with one another, assume such a right for themselves.

8. The Soviet Government states that the Soviet-Manchurian conflict can only be settled by means of direct negotiations between the USSR and China on the basis of conditions known to China and already accepted by the Mukden Government, and that it cannot allow any interference in these negotiations or in the conflict.

In conclusion the Soviet Government cannot help expressing its astonishment that the Government of the United States, which at its own desire has no official relations with the Government of the Soviet Union, finds it possible to approach the Soviet Government with advice and 'instructions.'

— Document No. 23 —

# STALIN'S REPORT, DECEMBER 3, 1927[24]

*The following passage from Stalin's report to the XV Party Congress, at the end of 1927, shows how he insisted in maintaining, as the period of the First Five Year Plan approached, that Europe was entering upon a new revolutionary phase. Precisely this proposition was bitterly challenged by Bukharin and other members of the Right opposition, who considered that capitalism was undergoing a stage of temporary stabilization.*

We have all the symptoms of an intense crisis and growing instability in world capitalism. If the temporary postwar crisis of 1920-21, with all its chaos within capitalist countries and the break-up of their foreign relations, has given way to a period of partial stabilization, nonetheless the general and main crisis of capitalism, resulting from the victorious October Revolution and the separation of the U.S.S.R. from the world capitalist system, is not only not overcome but is becoming more intense, shattering the very foundations of world capitalism. Stabilization, far from ameliorating this main crisis, has abetted it. The growing struggle for markets, the need of new spheres of influence and [therefore] of a new partition of the world, the failure of bourgeois pacifism and the League of Nations, the feverish work to form new coalitions for a possible new war, the frantic growth of armaments, the brutal oppression of the working class and the colonial countries, the growth of the revolutionary movement in the colonies and throughout Europe, the

[24] Eudin and Fisher, *op. cit.*, pp. 407-408.

growing authority of the Comintern throughout the world, and finally, the consolidation of the Soviet Union's power and its authority among the workers of Europe and the toiling masses of the colonial countries—these are the facts that shatter the very foundations of world capitalism.

The stabilization of capitalism is becoming more and more rotten and unstable.

If two years ago we had to speak about an ebb of the revolutionary wave in Europe, we now have every ground for claiming that Europe is definitely entering a phase of new revolutionary upheaval. I do not speak here of the colonial and dependent countries, where the situation of the imperialists is becoming more and more catastrophic.

Events have shattered the capitalists' hope that the U.S.S.R. would be tamed and its authority decline among the workers of Europe and the toiling masses of the colonial countries. The U.S.S.R. is growing, and growing toward socialism. Its influence among the workers and peasants throughout the world spreads and strengthens. The very existence of the U.S.S.R. as a country engaged in establishing socialism helps demoralize world imperialism and undermine its stability in both Europe and the colonial countries. The U.S.S.R. is definitely becoming a symbol for the working class of Europe and the oppressed colonial peoples.

Therefore, in order to clear the ground for future imperialist wars, to choke its "own" working class more thoroughly and muzzle its "own" colonies to strengthen its rear, capitalism must first of all (so the bourgeois policy makers believe) muzzle the U.S.S.R., the heart and nursery of revolution and at the same time one of the greatest markets for capitalist countries. Hence the revival of interventionist tendencies among the imperialists, and of the policy of isolating and encircling the U.S.S.R., the policy of preparing for war against the U.S.S.R.

The strengthening of interventionist tendencies in the imperialist camp and the menace of war against the U.S.S.R. is one of the main characteristics of the present situation.

## — Document No. 24 —

# STALIN'S SPEECH, APRIL 22, 1929[25]

*This passage, from a speech given by Stalin at the plenary session of the Central Committee and Central Control Commission of the Russian Communist Party on April 22, 1929, will illustrate the extent to which, at that time, the question of the trend of the capitalist world—whether toward disintegration or stabilization—still constituted a central issue of controversy between Stalin and the Right opposition.*

The first question concerns the character of the stabilization of capitalism. One gets from Bukharin's theses the impression that nothing new, nothing which could be disrupting the stabilization of capitalism, is happening at the present moment, that, on the contrary, capitalism is in process of reconstruction and is basically holding its own more or less firmly. Plainly the delegation of the All-Union Communist Party (of Bolsheviki) [ACP(B)] cannot agree with such an interpretation of the so-called third period, that is of the period which we are now experiencing. The delegation cannot agree with this, since the maintenance of such an interpretation of the third period could give our critics grounds for saying that we are adopting the point of view of the so-called "recovery" of capitalism, that is the point of view of Hilferding, a point of view which we, as communists, cannot take. In view of this the delegation of the ACP(B) introduced an alteration making it clear that the capitalist

[25] Stalin, *op. cit.*, Vol. 12 (1949), pp. 20-21.

stabilization is not a firm one and cannot be a firm one, that it is being disrupted and will continue to be disrupted by the course of events, in view of the sharpening of the crisis of world capitalism.

This question, comrades, has decisive importance for the [foreign] sections of the Comintern. Whether the stabilization of capitalism is breaking up or is being consolidated—on this question rests the entire orientation of the communist parties in their daily political work. Whether we are experiencing a period of decline in the revolutionary movement, a period of the simple collection of one's strength, or whether we are experiencing a period of the growth of the conditions for a new wave of revolutionary enthusiasm, a period of the preparation of the working class for the coming class struggles—on this depends the tactical orientation of the communist parties. The alteration introduced by the ACP(B) and subsequently accepted by the Congress is useful precisely because it gives a clear orientation towards the second of these two prospects, towards the prospect of the growth of the conditions for a new wave of revolutionary enthusiasm.

## — Document No. 25 —

# STALIN'S REPORT, JUNE 27, 1930[26]

*By the middle of 1930, the world economic crisis, while not yet at its peak, had assumed such dimensions as to constitute a major factor in international life. The*

[26] *Ibid.*, pp. 247, 254-257.

*intense and hopeful interest with which Moscow viewed this development, as also the skillful manner in which Stalin exploited it to support his existing line on foreign policy, are shown in the following passages from the political report which he presented to the XVI Party Congress on June 27, 1930.*

✓ ✓ ✓

2. The sharpening of the contradictions of capitalism.

. . .

Such is the state of the basic contradictions of world capitalism, now aggravated in the extreme by the world economic crisis.

To what do these facts attest?

They indicate that the stabilization of capitalism is coming to an end.

They indicate that the new wave of the revolutionary movement of the masses will grow with new force.

They indicate that the world economic crisis will turn into a political crisis in a number of countries.

This means, in the first place, that the bourgeoisie will seek escape from its difficulties in a further fascistization in the field of domestic policy, utilizing for this all the reactionary forces, including the social-democrats. This means, secondly, that the bourgeoisie will seek escape from its difficulties, on the plane of foreign policy, in a new imperialist war.

This means, finally, that the proletariat, struggling against capitalist exploitation and against the danger of war, will seek *its* way out by revolution.

. . .

Thus we see two categories of factors and two separate tendencies operating in opposite directions, to wit:

1. The policy of the disruption of the economic ties of the U.S.S.R. with capitalist countries; provocative sallies against the U.S.S.R.; overt and covert work in preparation for intervention against the U.S.S.R. These are factors threatening the international position of the U.S.S.R. It is these factors which explain such things as the break with the U.S.S.R. by the Conservative cabinet in England, the seizure of the Chinese-Eastern Railway by the Chinese militarists, the financial blockade of the

U.S.S.R., the "crusade" against the U.S.S.R. by the clergy headed by the Pope, the recruitment of our specialists for sabotage by the agents of foreign states, the setting off of explosions and fires such as those that were brought about by certain employees of the Lena-Gold Fields Company, attempts on the lives of representatives of the U.S.S.R. (Poland), harassment of our export trade (U.S.A., Poland), etc.

2. Sympathy and support for the U.S.S.R. on the part of the workers of capitalist countries; the growth of the economic and political might of the U.S.S.R.; the growth of the defense capability of the U.S.S.R.; the policy of peace pursued undeviatingly by the Soviet regime. These are factors strengthening the international position of the U.S.S.R. It is these factors that explain such things as the successful liquidation of the conflict over the Chinese-Eastern Railway, the re-establishment of relations with Great Britain, the growth of economic ties with capitalist countries, etc.

The present international position of the U.S.S.R. is determined by the struggle between these factors.

# — Document No. 26 —

## *PRAVDA* EDITORIAL, NOVEMBER 11, 1930[27]

*One of the outstanding characteristics of the Soviet propaganda machine is the incessant use of repetition. This being so, significant expressions of Soviet official thought are often to be found not in any single authoritative document but in the general flow of material put out by the Soviet press and other media under the control of the ideological and agitation authorities of the Party. The following excerpt from a* Pravda *editorial in November 1930 was characteristic of a volume of similar material of this sort which appeared around that time in connection with the "Industrial Party" trial.*

*By "wreckers" the* Pravda *means the accused at the trial, and others like them, the effort plainly being to suggest that there was within the Soviet Union a widespread network of persons, inspired by Stalin's political opponents within Russia, and devoted to sabotaging Soviet economy for the benefit of hostile governments.*

The possibility of a return to the past by means purely of [exploiting] internal forces [within the Soviet Union] faded from reality and the wreckers devoted themselves entirely to the preparation of an attack by international capitalism on the Soviet Union. They were prepared to go to the limit—to war, to famine, to the ruin of the country, to the cession of portions of its territory to foreign states, if only the old order could be restored.

[27] *Pravda,* November 11, 1930.

The wreckers became the military and espionage network of international capitalism within the Soviet Union. They intended to develop activities directed to the demoralization of the Red Army, they were ready to undertake diversionists acts. . . . The immediate leader of the counterrevolutionary work became the aggressive warmongering imperialism of France. It was this that guided the hands of the wreckers.

The preliminary testimony shows that Poincaré-la-Guerre and other dyed-in-the-wool representatives of French imperialism were the immediate leaders of the counterrevolutionary wreckers. The wreckers were humble servants in the hands of the mortal enemies of the Soviet Union.

The wreckers miscalculated. Their efforts to create within the country an economic crisis which would arouse the dissatisfaction of the masses and would thereby prepare the ground for intervention proved futile. *The U.S.S.R. achieved exceptional success in the building of socialism. . . .*

## — Document No. 27 —

# STALIN'S REPORT, JANUARY 26, 1934[28]

*In his report to the XVII Party Congress, Stalin cites recognition by the United States as one of the two main successes of Soviet diplomacy at that time. The final passage about Japan is included here for its value as an indication of the close association in Stalin's mind between American recognition and the problem of Soviet-Japanese relations.*

[28] Degras, *Soviet Documents on Foreign Policy, op. cit.,* Vol. III, *1933-1941* (London, 1953), pp. 69, 71-72. Published by Oxford University Press on behalf of the Royal Institute of International Affairs; used by permission.

✓ ✓ ✓

Of the many facts reflecting the successes of the peace policy of the USSR, two facts of indisputably material significance should be singled out.

1. . . .

2. Secondly, I have in mind the restoration of normal relations between the USSR and the United States. There cannot be any doubt that this act is of great significance for the whole system of international relations. It is not only that it improves the chances of preserving peace, and that it improves the relations between the two countries, strengthens commercial intercourse between them, and creates a base for their mutual collaboration. The point is that it is a landmark between the old position, when in various countries the United States was regarded as the champion of every kind of anti-Soviet trend, and the new position, when the championship has been voluntarily dropped, to the mutual advantage of both countries.

. . .

Nor can we lose sight of the relations between the USSR and Japan, which stand in need of very considerable improvement. Japan's refusal to conclude a pact of non-aggression, of which Japan stands in no less need than the USSR, once again emphasizes the fact that all is not well in our relations. The same must be said of the rupture of negotiations concerning the Chinese Eastern Railway, due to no fault of the USSR; and also of the outrageous actions of the Japanese agents on the CER, the illegal arrest of Soviet employees on the CER, etc. All this apart from the fact that one section of the military in Japan, with the avowed approval of another section of the military, is openly advocating in the press the necessity for a war against the USSR and the seizure of the Maritime Province; while the Government of Japan, instead of calling these instigators of war to order, pretends that it has nothing to do with the matter. It is not difficult to understand that such circumstances cannot but create an atmosphere of uneasiness and uncertainty. Of course, we will persistently continue our policy of peace and will strive to bring about an improvement in our relations with Japan, because we want to improve these relations. But it does not depend entirely upon us. That is why we must at the same time take all measures to guard our country against surprises, and be prepared to defend it in the event of attack.

## — Document No. 28 —

# STALIN'S *VOPROSY LENINIZMA*[29]

*In the following excerpt, Stalin was analyzing what he claimed to be the motives of the western powers in refusing to intervene in Spain. Actually, he was putting here into the minds of his adversaries the central concept of the political strategy that dominated his activity both as a statesman and as an aspirant for supreme power within the Russian communist movement. It is an admirable description of what he hoped to accomplish by concluding a nonaggression pact with Germany in 1939 and thus practicing a policy of "nonintervention" with relation to the German-Polish war.*

✓ ✓ ✓

The policy of non-intervention means the abetting of aggression, of unleashing war—consequently the transformation of war into world war. There shines through the policy of non-intervention the desire not to hinder the aggressors in the performance of their dirty work, not to hinder Japan, let us say, from getting tangled in a war with China or, better still, with the Soviet Union, not to hinder Germany, let us say, from getting bogged down in European matters or becoming entangled in a war with the Soviet Union, to permit all the participants

[29] Quoted in *Bolshaya Sovyetskaya entsiklopediya* (Great Soviet Encyclopedia), 2nd Edition (Moscow 1950), Vol. 19, p. 139.

in a war to become deeply bogged down in the mire of the war, to encourage them surreptitiously in this direction, to let them weaken and exhaust each other, and then, when they are sufficiently weakened, to come onto the scene with fresh forces, to come on, of course, "in the interests of peace," and to dictate one's terms to the weakened participants in the war. . . .

## — Document No. 29 —

# LITVINOV'S SPEECH IN LENINGRAD, JUNE 23, 1938[30]

*Here Litvinov, speaking at an election meeting in June 1938, gives a brief statement of the Soviet relationship to the Spanish civil war on the overt, official level. He explains why the Soviet government at one time formally adhered to the nonintervention arrangements.*

In the interests of international co-operation, we joined in the agreement for non-intervention in Spanish affairs. We never believed the legend that the absence of such an agreement created a threat to peace. Nor did we consider that to supply the lawful Spanish Government with arms against a handful of insurgent generals was intervention in Spanish affairs. Nevertheless, in the interests of international solidarity, and convinced that the Spanish Government could with its own forces cope with the insurgents if they were deprived of external help, we signed the agreement and entered the London committee, on the assumption that it would, at least, really guarantee

[30] Degras, *Soviet Documents . . .*, Vol. III, *op. cit.*, p. 289.

complete non-intervention. From the very outset we did not have excessive faith in the signatures of the fascist countries which openly mock at obligations and treaties, and hence we introduced a proposal to guarantee effective control with the help of the French and British navies. I am convinced that the adoption of our proposal would not only have put an end to the war in Spain, without arousing any international complications, but would have meant a shattering defeat to aggression in general. Unfortunately, those States whose interests, as I pointed out before, are most threatened by the Italo-German intervention in Spain, preferred the tactics of countenancing the aggressors, and made endless concessions to them. If the aggressors dislike a control, then it is cancelled; if they propose another system of control more advantageous to them, it is adopted. They demand belligerent rights for Franco, and these rights are promised him. Under such conditions the committee not only failed completely to ensure non-intervention, it is listing more and more to Franco's side. Our role in the committee now resolves itself to attempts to straighten out this list to the best of our ability, and at least to prevent the intervention of the committee itself in Spanish affairs on Franco's side. . . .

## — Document No. 30 —

# STALIN'S REPORT, MARCH 10, 1939[31]

*The following is the kernel of Stalin's famous speech on March 10, 1939 to the XVIII Party Congress, in which he made clear his suspicion that the western powers were*

[31] *Foreign Relations, The Soviet Union, 1933-1939* (Washington 1952), p. 741.

*trying to involve Russia in a war with Germany for their own benefit, and his determination to remain aloof. Stalin is said to have confirmed personally to von Ribbentrop, at their August meeting, that this passage was intended as a sign to Hitler that the Soviet government considered a German-Soviet rapprochement to be both possible and desirable.*[32]

The foreign policy of the Soviet Union is clear and comprehensible: (1) We stand for peace and for the strengthening of business likely to affect ties with all countries. We stand and will stand on that position insofar as these countries will maintain such relations with the Soviet Union and insofar as they do not attempt to infringe the interests of our country. (2) We stand for peaceful, close, and good neighborly relations with all neighboring countries which have a common frontier with the Soviet Union. We stand and will stand on that position insofar as these countries will maintain such relations with the Soviet Union and insofar as they do not attempt to infringe directly or indirectly the interests, integrity, and inviolability, of the frontiers of the Soviet state. (3) We stand for the support of peoples who have become victims of aggression and who are struggling for the independence of their fatherland. (4) We do not fear threats on the part of aggressors and are ready to answer with redoubled blow a blow from the incendiaries of war attempting to infringe the inviolability of the Soviet frontiers. Such is the foreign policy of the Soviet Union. In its foreign policy the Soviet Union bases itself first, on its growing economic, political, and cultural strength; second, on the moral and political

[32] See A. Rossi, *Le Pacte Germano-Soviétique: L'Histoire et la Mythe* (Paris, 1954), p. 46. I have taken the liberty of correcting the State Department translation in one place; instead of the phrase "*provocateurs* of war, who are accustomed to using others as cats' paws," I have used the more direct translation, "who are accustomed to having others pull the chestnuts out of the fire for them." It was precisely this reference to chestnuts which constituted the plainest hint to the Germans and which is most frequently referred to by historians of this period.

unity of our Soviet social system; third, on the friendships of the peoples of our country; fourth, on its Red Army and Navy; fifth, on its policy of peace; sixth, on the moral support of the workers of all countries who are vitally interested in the preservation of peace; seventh, in the good sense of those countries who are not interested for one or another reason in the violation of peace. The tasks of our Party in the realm of foreign policy are: (1) to continue in the future as well as to carry on the policy of peace and of strengthening of business-like ties with all countries; (2) to observe caution and not to permit our country to be drawn into a conflict by the *provocateurs* of war, who are accustomed to having others pull the chestnuts out of the fire for them; (3) to strengthen in every way the military might of our Red army and naval Red fleet; (4) to strengthen the international ties of friendship with the toilers of all countries who are interested in peace and in friendship between peoples.

## — Document No. 31 —

# GERMAN-SOVIET TREATY OF NONAGGRESSION[33]

*The following is the text of the German-Soviet Nonaggression Pact signed by von Ribbentrop and Molotov in Moscow on August 23, 1939, together with the secret protocol by which it was accompanied.*

[33] *Nazi-Soviet Relations 1939-1941: Documents from the Archives of the German Foreign Office* (edited by Raymond James Sontag and James Stuart Beddie), Department of State, 1948, pp. 76-78.

The Government of the German Reich and the Government of the Union of Soviet Socialist Republics desirous of strengthening the cause of peace between Germany and the U.S.S.R., and proceeding from the fundamental provisions of the Neutrality Agreement concluded in April 1926 between Germany and the U.S.S.R., have reached the following agreement:

ARTICLE I. Both High Contracting Parties obligate themselves to desist from any act of violence, any aggressive action, and any attack on each other, either individually or jointly with other powers.

ARTICLE II. Should one of the High Contracting Parties become the object of belligerent action by a third power, the other High Contracting Party shall in no manner lend its support to this third power.

ARTICLE III. The Governments of the two High Contracting Parties shall in the future maintain continual contact with one another for the purpose of consultation in order to exchange information on problems affecting their common interests.

ARTICLE IV. Neither of the two High Contracting Parties shall participate in any grouping of powers whatsoever that is directly or indirectly aimed at the other party.

ARTICLE V. Should disputes or conflicts arise between the High Contracting Parties over problems of one kind or another, both parties shall settle these disputes or conflicts exclusively through friendly exchange of opinion or, if necessary, through the establishment of arbitration commissions.

ARTICLE VI. The present treaty is concluded for a period of ten years, with the proviso that, in so far as one of the High Contracting Parties does not denounce it one year prior to the expiration of this period, the validity of this treaty shall automatically be extended for another five years.

ARTICLE VII. The present treaty shall be ratified within the shortest possible time. The ratifications shall be exchanged in Berlin. The agreement shall enter into force as soon as it is signed.

. . .

[Signatures]

## SECRET ADDITIONAL PROTOCOL

On the occasion of the signature of the Nonaggression Pact between the German Reich and the Union of Socialist Soviet Republics the undersigned plenipotentiaries of each of the two parties discussed in strictly confidential conversations the question of the boundary of their respective spheres of influence in Eastern Europe. These conversations led to the following conclusions:

1. In the event of a territorial and political rearrangement in the areas belonging to the Baltic States (Finland, Estonia, Latvia, Lithuania), the northern boundary of Lithuania shall represent the boundary of the spheres of influence of Germany and the U.S.S.R. In this connection the interest of Lithuania in the Vilna area is recognized by each party.

2. In the event of a territorial and political rearrangement of the areas belonging to the Polish state the spheres of influence of Germany and the U.S.S.R. shall be bounded approximately by the line of the rivers Narew, Vistula, and San.

The question of whether the interests of both parties make desirable the maintenance of an independent Polish state and how such a state should be bounded can only be definitely determined in the course of further political developments.

In any event both Governments will resolve this question by means of a friendly agreement.

3. With regard to Southeastern Europe attention is called by the Soviet side to its interest in Bessarabia. The German side declares its complete political disinterestedness in these areas.

4. This protocol shall be treated by both parties as strictly secret.

. . .

[Signatures]

## — Document No. 32 —

# SOVIET STATEMENT TO POLAND, SEPTEMBER 17, 1939[34]

*The following is the communication handed to the Polish Ambassador in Moscow at 3:00 a.m., on September 17, 1939, by the Deputy Commissar for Foreign Affairs, Mr. Vladimir Potemkin, in connection with the advance (which had already begun) of Soviet forces into Poland. The statement was released to the press the same day.*

✓ ✓ ✓

The Polish-German War has revealed the internal bankruptcy of the Polish State. During the course of ten days' hostilities Poland has lost all her industrial areas and cultural centres. Warsaw no longer exists as the capital of Poland. The Polish Government has disintegrated, and no longer shows any sign of life. This means that the Polish State and its Government have, in fact, ceased to exist. Therefore the Agreements concluded between the U.S.S.R. and Poland have ceased to operate. Left to her own devices and bereft of leadership, Poland has become a suitable field for all manner of hazards and surprises, which may constitute a threat to the U.S.S.R. For these reasons the Soviet Government, which hitherto has preserved neutrality, cannot any longer observe a neutral attitude towards these facts.

The Soviet Government further cannot view with in-

[34] *Official Documents concerning Polish-German and Polish-Soviet Relations 1933-1939* (London, n.d.), pp. 189-190.

difference the fact that the kindred Ukrainian and White Russian people, who live on Polish territory and who are at the mercy of fate, are left defenceless.

In these circumstances, the Soviet Government has directed the High Command of the Red Army to order the troops to cross the frontier and to take under their protection the life and property of the population of Western Ukraine and Western White Russia.

At the same time, the Soviet Government proposes to take all measures to extricate the Polish people from the unfortunate war into which they were dragged by their unwise leaders, and to enable them to live a peaceful life.

## — Document No. 33 —

# GERMAN-SOVIET TREATY, SEPTEMBER 28, 1939[35]

*The following is the text of the agreement concluded between the German and Soviet governments on the occasion of Ribbentrop's second visit to Moscow, on September 28, 1939. It provides for an alteration of the previous line of demarcation in Poland, assigns Lithuania to the Soviet sphere, and envisages the repatriation to Germany of people of German descent residing in the territories on the Soviet side of the line.*

✓ ✓ ✓

The Government of the German Reich and the Government of the U.S.S.R. consider it as exclusively their task, after the collapse of the former Polish state, to reestablish peace and order in these territories and to assure to the peoples living there a peaceful life in keeping with

[35] *Nazi-Soviet Relations, op. cit.,* pp. 105-107.

their national character. To this end, they have agreed upon the following:

ARTICLE I. The Government of the German Reich and the Government of the U.S.S.R. determine as the boundary of their respective national interests in the territory of the former Polish state the line marked on the attached map, which shall be described in more detail in a supplementary protocol.

ARTICLE II. Both parties recognize the boundary of the respective national interests established in article I as definitive and shall reject any interference of third powers in this settlement.

ARTICLE III. The necessary reorganization of public administration will be effected in the areas west of the line specified in article I by the Government of the German Reich, in the areas east of this line by the Government of the U.S.S.R.

ARTICLE IV. The Government of the German Reich and the Government of the U.S.S.R. regard this settlement as a firm foundation for a progressive development of the friendly relations between their peoples.

ARTICLE V. This treaty shall be ratified and the ratifications shall be exchanged in Berlin as soon as possible. The treaty becomes effective upon signature.

. . .

[Signatures]

## CONFIDENTIAL PROTOCOL

The Government of the U.S.S.R. shall place no obstacles in the way of Reich nationals and other persons of German descent residing in the territories under its jurisdiction, if they desire to migrate to Germany or to the territories under German jurisdiction. It agrees that such removals shall be carried out by agents of the Government of the Reich in cooperation with the competent local authorities and that the property rights of the emigrants shall be protected.

A corresponding obligation is assumed by the Government of the German Reich in respect to the persons of Ukrainian or White Russian descent residing in the territories under its jurisdiction.

. . .

[Signatures]

### SECRET SUPPLEMENTARY PROTOCOL

The undersigned Plenipotentiaries declare the agreement of the Government of the German Reich and the Government of the U.S.S.R. upon the following:

The Secret Supplementary Protocol signed on August 23, 1939, shall be amended in item 1 to the effect that the territory of the Lithuanian state falls to the sphere of influence of the U.S.S.R., while, on the other hand, the province of Lublin and parts of the province of Warsaw fall to the sphere of influence of Germany (cf. the map attached to the Boundary and Friendship Treaty signed today). As soon as the Government of the U.S.S.R. shall take special measures on Lithuanian territory to protect its interests, the present German-Lithuanian border, for the purpose of a natural and simple boundary delineation, shall be rectified in such a way that the Lithuanian territory situated to the southwest of the line marked on the attached map shall fall to Germany.

Further it is declared that the economic agreements now in force between Germany and Lithuania shall not be affected by the measures of the Soviet Union referred to above.

. . .

[Signatures]

### SECRET SUPPLEMENTARY PROTOCOL

The undersigned plenipotentiaries, on concluding the German-Russian Boundary and Friendship Treaty, have declared their agreement upon the following:

Both parties will tolerate in their territories no Polish agitation which affects the territories of the other party. They will suppress in their territories all beginnings of such agitation and inform each other concerning suitable measures for this purpose.

. . .

[Signatures]

## — Document No. 34 —

# SOVIET NOTE TO GERMANY, NOVEMBER 25, 1940[36]

*These were the stiff terms put by the Soviet government to the German government in the fall of 1940, as a price for Russia's adherence to the Three-Power Pact. It was their unacceptability to Hitler which clinched his decision to undertake the invasion of Russia.*

✓ ✓ ✓

The Soviet Government is prepared to accept the draft of the Four Power Pact which the Reich Foreign Minister outlined in the conversation of November 13, regarding political collaboration and reciprocal economic support subject to the following conditions:

1) Provided that the German troops are immediately withdrawn from Finland, which, under the compact of 1939, belongs to the Soviet Union's sphere of influence. At the same time the Soviet Union undertakes to ensure peaceful relations with Finland and to protect German economic interests in Finland (export of lumber and nickel).

2) Provided that within the next few months the security of the Soviet Union in the Straits is assured by the conclusion of a mutual assistance pact between the Soviet Union and Bulgaria, which geographically is situated inside the security zone of the Black Sea boundaries of the Soviet Union, and by the establishment of a base for land and naval forces of the U.S.S.R. within range of the Bosporus and the Dardanelles by means of a long-term lease.

[36] *Ibid.*, pp. 258-259.

3) Provided that the area south of Batum and Baku in the general direction of the Persian Gulf is recognized as the center of the aspirations of the Soviet Union.

4) Provided that Japan renounces her rights to concessions for coal and oil in Northern Sakhalin.

In accordance with the foregoing, the draft of the protocol concerning the delimitation of the spheres of influence as outlined by the Reich Foreign Minister would have to be amended so as to stipulate the focal point of the aspirations of the Soviet Union south of Batum and Baku in the general direction of the Persian Gulf.

Likewise, the draft of the protocol or agreement between Germany, Italy, and the Soviet Union with respect to Turkey should be amended so as to guarantee a base for light naval and land forces of the U.S.S.R. on the Bosporus and the Dardanelles by means of a long-term lease, including—in case Turkey declares herself willing to join the Four Power Pact—a guarantee of the independence and of the territory of Turkey by the three countries named.

This protocol should provide that in case Turkey refuses to join the Four Powers, Germany, Italy, and the Soviet Union agree to work out and to carry through the required military and diplomatic measures, and a separate agreement to this effect should be concluded.

Furthermore there should be agreement upon:

*a*) a third secret protocol between Germany and the Soviet Union concerning Finland (see Point I above).

*b*) a fourth secret protocol between Japan and the Soviet Union concerning the renunciation by Japan of the oil and coal concession in Northern Sakhalin (in return for an adequate compensation).

*c*) a fifth secret protocol between Germany, the Soviet Union, and Italy, recognizing that Bulgaria is geographically located inside the security zone of the Black Sea boundaries of the Soviet Union and that it is therefore a political necessity that a mutual assistance pact be concluded between the Soviet Union and Bulgaria, which in no way shall affect the internal regime of Bulgaria, her sovereignty or independence.

# A SELECTED BIBLIOGRAPHY

Beloff, Max, *The Foreign Policy of Soviet Russia 1929-1941* (2 vols.), London and New York, 1947-1949.

——, *Soviet Policy in the Far East 1944-1951*, London and New York, 1953.

Borkenau, Franz, *European Communism*, New York, 1953.

Böttcher, Helmuth M., *Walther Rathenau*, Bonn, 1958.

Brandt, Conrad, *Stalin's Failure in China*, Cambridge, 1958.

Buell, Raymond Leslie, *Poland: Key to Europe*, London, 1939.

Carr, Edward Hallett, *German-Soviet Relations Between the Two World Wars, 1919-1939*, Baltimore, 1951.

——, *A History of Soviet Russia* (6 vols.), London and New York, 1950-1960.

——, *The Soviet Impact on the Western World*, London and New York, 1947.

Cattell, David T., *Communism and the Spanish Civil War*, Berkeley, California, 1955.

——, *Soviet Diplomacy and the Spanish Civil War*, Berkeley, California, 1957.

Coates, W. P. and Zelda K., *Armed Intervention in Russia*, London, 1935.

——, *A History of Anglo-Soviet Relations* (2 vols.), London, 1943, 1958.

Colodny, Robert Garland, *The Struggle for Madrid*, New York, 1958.

Coulondre, Robert, *De Staline à Hitler*, Paris, 1950.

Dallin, David J., *The Big Three*, New Haven, 1945.

——, *Soviet Russia and the Far East*, New Haven, 1948.

——, *Soviet Russia's Foreign Policy*, New Haven, 1942.

Degras, Jane, Ed., *The Communist International 1919-1943*, Vol. I, London and New York, 1956.

——, *Soviet Documents on Foreign Policy* (3 vols.), London and New York, 1951-1953.

Deutscher, Isaac, *The Prophet Armed: Trotsky 1879-1921,* New York and London, 1954.

——, *The Prophet Unarmed: Trotsky, 1921-1929,* New York and London, 1959.

——, *Stalin: A Political Biography,* New York and London, 1949.

Eudin, Xenia Joukoff and North, Robert, *Soviet Russia and the East 1920-1927,* Stanford, California, 1957.

Eudin, Xenia Joukoff and Fisher, Harold H., *Soviet Russia and the West 1920-1927,* Stanford, California, 1957.

Fischer, Louis, *Men and Politics,* New York, 1941.

——, *The Soviets in World Affairs* (2 vols.), Princeton, 1951.

Fischer, Ruth, *Stalin and German Communism,* Cambridge, 1948.

Fisher, H. H., *The Famine in Soviet Russia,* New York, 1927.

Freund, Gerald, *Unholy Alliance,* New York, 1957.

Gankin, Olga Hess, and Fisher, H. H., *The Bolsheviks and the World War,* Stanford, California, 1940.

German Foreign Office, *Documents on the Events Preceding the Outbreak of the War,* Berlin and New York, 1939-40.

Graubard, Stephen Richards, *British Labour and the Russian Revolution 1917-1924,* London, 1956.

Hilger, Gustav and Meyer, Alfred G., *The Incompatible Allies,* New York, 1953.

James, C. L. R., *World Revolution 1917-1936,* London, 1957.

Kessler, Harry Graf, *Walter Rathenau,* Berlin-Grunewald, 1928.

Kleist, Peter, *Zwischen Hitler und Stalin,* Bonn, 1950.

Kochan, Lionel, *Russia and the Weimar Republic,* Cambridge, England, 1954.

Langer, William L., and Gleason, S. Everett, *The Challenge to Isolation 1937-1940,* New York, 1952.

——, *The Undeclared War 1940-1941,* New York, 1953.

Lenin, V. I., *Sochineniya* (35 vols.), Moscow, 1950-1952.

Lundin, C. Leonard, *Finland in the Second World War,* Bloomington, Indiana, 1957.

Mazour, Anatole G., *Finland between East and West,* Princeton, 1956.

McLane, Charles B., *Soviet Policy and the Chinese Communists 1931-1946,* New York, 1958.

Ministry of Foreign Affairs of the U.S.S.R., *Documents and Materials Relating to the Eve of the Second World War* (2 vols.), Moscow, 1948.

——, *Dokumenty vneshnyei politiki SSSR* (2 vols.), Moscow, 1957-1958.

*Nazi-Soviet Relations 1939-1941* (Raymond J. Sontag and James S. Beddie, Editors), Washington, D.C., 1948.

Nicolson, Harold, *Curzon: The Last Phase 1919-1925,* New York, 1939.

——, *Peacemaking 1919,* London, 1937.

Norton, Henry Kittredge, *China and the Powers,* New York, 1927.

Rossi, A., *Deux Ans d'Alliance Germano-Soviétique, Aout 1939-Juin 1941,* Paris, 1949.

——, *Le Pacte Germano-Soviétique,* Paris, 1954.

Rubinstein, Alvin Z., Ed., *The Foreign Policy of the Soviet Union,* New York, 1960.

Schieder, Theodor, *Die Probleme des Rapallo-Vertrags,* Köln and Opladen, 1955.

Schlesinger, Arthur M. Jr., *The Crisis of the Old Order 1919-1933,* London, 1957.

Schmidt, Paul, *Statist auf diplomatischer Bühne 1923-45,* Bonn, 1954.

Spector, Ivar, *The Soviet Union and the Muslim World, 1917-1958,* Seattle, 1959.

Stalin, I. V., *Sochineniya* (13 vols.), Moscow, 1947-52.

Stern-Rubarth, Edgar, *Graf Brockdorff-Rantzau,* Berlin, 1929.

Tikhomirov, M., *Vneshnaya politika Sovetskogo Soyuza,* Moscow, 1940.

Trotsky, Leon, *Problems of the Chinese Revolution,* New York, 1932.

von Blücher, Wipert, *Deutschlands weg nach Rapallo,* Wiesbaden, 1951.

von Dirksen, Herbert, *Moskau Tokio London,* Stuttgart, 1950.

Whiting, Allen S., *Soviet Policies in China 1917-1924,* New York, 1953.

Woodward, E. L., and Butler, Rohan, Eds., *Documents on British Foreign Policy* (selected volumes), London, 1949– ——.

Wu, Aitchen K., *China and the Soviet Union,* New York, 1950.

# INDEX

043 000